DESIGN AND PERFORMANCE OF BIOMETRIC SYSTEM

COMPUTER SCIENCE, TECHNOLOGY AND APPLICATIONS

Additional books in this series can be found on Nova's website at:

https://www.novapublishers.com/catalog/index.php?cPath=23_29&seriesp
=Computer%20Science%2C%20Technology%20and%20Applications&sort=
2a&page=1

Additional e-books in this series can be found on Nova's website at:

https://www.novapublishers.com/catalog/index.php?cPath=23_29&seriesp
e=Computer+Science%2C+Technology+and+Applications

COMPUTER SCIENCE, TECHNOLOGY AND APPLICATIONS

DESIGN AND PERFORMANCE OF BIOMETRIC SYSTEM

JOHN T. ELSWORTH
EDITOR

Nova Science Publishers, Inc.
New York

Copyright © 2010 by Nova Science Publishers, Inc.

For permission to use material from this book please contact us:
Telephone 631-231-7269; Fax 631-231-8175
Web Site: http://www.novapublishers.com

NOTICE TO THE READER

The Publisher has taken reasonable care in the preparation of this book, but makes no expressed or implied warranty of any kind and assumes no responsibility for any errors or omissions. No liability is assumed for incidental or consequential damages in connection with or arising out of information contained in this book. The Publisher shall not be liable for any special, consequential, or exemplary damages resulting, in whole or in part, from the readers' use of, or reliance upon, this material. Any parts of this book based on government reports are so indicated and copyright is claimed for those parts to the extent applicable to compilations of such works.

Independent verification should be sought for any data, advice or recommendations contained in this book. In addition, no responsibility is assumed by the publisher for any injury and/or damage to persons or property arising from any methods, products, instructions, ideas or otherwise contained in this publication.

This publication is designed to provide accurate and authoritative information with regard to the subject matter covered herein. It is sold with the clear understanding that the Publisher is not engaged in rendering legal or any other professional services. If legal or any other expert assistance is required, the services of a competent person should be sought. FROM A DECLARATION OF PARTICIPANTS JOINTLY ADOPTED BY A COMMITTEE OF THE AMERICAN BAR ASSOCIATION AND A COMMITTEE OF PUBLISHERS.

LIBRARY OF CONGRESS CATALOGING-IN-PUBLICATION DATA

Available Upon Request

ISBN : 978-1-60692-978-0

Published by Nova Science Publishers, Inc. ✝ *New York*

CONTENTS

PREFACE

The use of biometrics to confirm personal identity has become a key component to our nation's security. And, as such, there is an escalating need to design and develop biometric systems which accurately and effectively identify individuals. To date, biometric technologies are the most definitive, real-time identity management tools currently available, yet many shortcomings of these tools have yet to be addressed. This book works to introduce designers to the concept of usability and showcase the ways in which a properly implemented user-centered design process can improve a system's effectiveness, and efficiency, and user satisfaction.

Chapter 1 - The requirements necessary for taking a successful face picture are fairly straightforward. The camera must be operational, and the subject must be illuminated sufficiently, facing the camera and in focus. Yet, a significant portion of the facial photographs taken at United States ports of entry are unusable for the purposes of automatic face recognition. In this paper, we consider the usability components of the face image capture process that contribute to the relatively high ratio of unusable images collected by United States Visitor and Immigrant Status Indicator Technology (US-VISIT). In addition, we introduce a general evaluation methodology—including the use of a simple image overlay—to quantify various characteristics of face imagery. The experimental context mimicked the point-of-entry environment, but with specific usability enhancements. The collected data suggests that these usability enhancements may be used to improve face image capture with the current equipment.

US-VISIT requested that the biometrics usability team at the National Institute of Standards and Technology (NIST) examine the current US-VISIT face image collection process to identify any usability and human factors that

may improve the existing face image capture process. As such this study did not address other technologies or technology solutions. This report presents the results of a study that examined five usability and human factors enhancements to the current US-VISIT collection process:

1. the camera should resemble a traditional camera;
2. the camera should click when the picture is taken to provide feedback to the traveler that the picture is being taken;
3. the camera should be used in portrait mode;
4. the operator should be facing the traveler and the monitor while positioning the camera and
5. provide some marking on the floor (such as footprints) to indicate to the traveler where to stand for the photograph.

The study was conducted as follows: first we visited and observed a representative operational setting (Dulles Airport) in order to understand the primary users and the context of use. Based on these observations we identified the 5 usability and human factors enhancements enumerated above that may improve the face image capture process. A usability study was designed that mimicked the operational process but incorporated the 5 enhancements and face images were collected from 300 participants. A visual inspection evaluation methodology based on an image overlay was used to quantify the various characteristics of face imagery based on the face image standards. Results from the visual inspection process compared favorably with preliminary automated face image quality metrics under development.

This report describes three main results. The enhancements were designed to address the extreme conditions or departures in the captured images. Implementing these enhancements resulted in:

1. 100 % of the images capturing a participant's face in contrast to the current US- VISIT collection
2. all of the participants were facing the camera -- this is a significant improvement to the process currently used at the ports of entry
3. additional improvement may be realized by using the face overlay guide proactively. By incorporating the overlay into the workstations the officers could use the guide to center the camera on the participant's face.

The recommended enhancements improved the overall captured images and can be implemented relatively easily and with relatively little cost. A follow-up study incorporating the overlay into the operators' workflow is underway.

Chapter 2 - This handbook provides a common understanding and vocabulary for usability to encourage communication between usability and biometric researchers and practitioners. It begins by examining the biometric collection process and the role of the user and user characteristics. We examine the concept of usability and how it is defined. We introduce the user-centered design process and the value of the process to the development of biometrics systems. The elements of the user centered design process including context of use, user and organizational requirements, design solutions, and evaluation techniques are defined and described. Finally a list of usability methods and techniques are elaborated.

In: Design and Performance of Biometric System   ISBN: 978-1-60692-978-0
Editor: John T. Elsworth   © 2010 Nova Science Publishers, Inc.

Chapter 1

ASSESSING FACE ACQUISITION

Mary Theofanos, Brian Stanton, Charles Sheppard, Ross Michaels, John Libert and Shahram Orandi

EXECUTIVE SUMMARY

The requirements necessary for taking a successful face picture are fairly straightforward. The camera must be operational, and the subject must be illuminated sufficiently, facing the camera and in focus. Yet, a significant portion of the facial photographs taken at United States ports of entry are unusable for the purposes of automatic face recognition. In this paper, we consider the usability components of the face image capture process that contribute to the relatively high ratio of unusable images collected by United States Visitor and Immigrant Status Indicator Technology (US-VISIT). In addition, we introduce a general evaluation methodology—including the use of a simple image overlay—to quantify various characteristics of face imagery. The experimental context mimicked the point-of-entry environment, but with specific usability enhancements. The collected data suggests that these usability enhancements may be used to improve face image capture with the current equipment.

US-VISIT requested that the biometrics usability team at the National Institute of Standards and Technology (NIST) examine the current US-VISIT face image collection process to identify any usability and human factors that may improve the existing face image capture process. As such this study did

not address other technologies or technology solutions. This report presents the results of a study that examined five usability and human factors enhancements to the current US-VISIT collection process:

1. the camera should resemble a traditional camera;
2. the camera should click when the picture is taken to provide feedback to the traveler that the picture is being taken;
3. the camera should be used in portrait mode;
4. the operator should be facing the traveler and the monitor while positioning the camera and
5. provide some marking on the floor (such as footprints) to indicate to the traveler where to stand for the photograph.

The study was conducted as follows: first we visited and observed a representative operational setting (Dulles Airport) in order to understand the primary users and the context of use. Based on these observations we identified the 5 usability and human factors enhancements enumerated above that may improve the face image capture process. A usability study was designed that mimicked the operational process but incorporated the 5 enhancements and face images were collected from 300 participants. A visual inspection evaluation methodology based on an image overlay was used to quantify the various characteristics of face imagery based on the face image standards. Results from the visual inspection process compared favorably with preliminary automated face image quality metrics under development.

This report describes three main results. The enhancements were designed to address the extreme conditions or departures in the captured images. Implementing these enhancements resulted in:

1. 100 % of the images capturing a participant's face in contrast to the current US- VISIT collection
2. all of the participants were facing the camera -- this is a significant improvement to the process currently used at the ports of entry
3. additional improvement may be realized by using the face overlay guide proactively. By incorporating the overlay into the workstations the officers could use the guide to center the camera on the participant's face.

The recommended enhancements improved the overall captured images and can be implemented relatively easily and with relatively little cost. A

follow-up study incorporating the overlay into the operators' workflow is underway.

1. INTRODUCTION

The Department of Homeland Security's (DHS) United States Visitor and Immigrant Status Indicator Technology (US-VISIT) program is a biometrically-enhanced identification system primarily situated at border points of entry such as airports and seaports. The US-VISIT program's goal is to advance the security of the United States and worldwide travel through information sharing and biometric solutions to identity management. The biometrics currently captured at US-VISIT primary inspection are fingerprints and a facial image. The fingerprint component of the system uses automated matching along with manual match verification. The face image capture process does not include automated face recognition but relies on human verifiable traveler history. Currently two flat index fingerprints are collected; however, as of 2008, the migration to a 10-print "slap" has already begun.

A face image quality assessment of airport ports of entry was performed in 2004 [1]. This assessment found that key factors for face recognition included geometric properties of pose, size, cropping, fish-eye effects and photometric properties of compression, backgrounds, and saturation. An evaluation of approximately 1 .5M facial images using manual inspection found that:

- The subject was frontal to the camera in only about 5 % of images, approximately 70 % of the images had a pose angle of greater than 10 degrees
- About 5 % of the images have some part of the face cropped out of the picture
- About 1 % of the images have blur (usually motion artifacts).

An automated inspection of the same facial images with a face recognition system found that 95 % of images with an interocular distance below 74 pixels. The system failed to find the eyes in 10.6 % of the images. Finally, 14 % of the images were deemed unsuitable for face recognition.

Figure 1. Sample Face Images

To summarize—the primary problem with the collected images is poor geometry: specifically pose, size, crop and distortion as illustrated in Figure 1 Sample Face Images.

1 Specific hardware and software products identified in this report were used in order to perform the evaluations described. In no case does such identification imply recommendation or endorsement by the National Institute of Standards and Technology, nor does it imply that the products and equipment identified are necessarily the best available for the purpose.

As the result of this assessment US-VISIT has embarked on a program for face image quality improvement. One aspect of this effort is the identification of usability and human factors issues that may impact face image capture. The National Institute of Standards and Technology's (NIST) usability and biometrics team was asked to identify any usability and human factors considerations that may improve the capture of face images at the airports.

2. OBSERVATION

2.1. Users and Context of Use

The International Organization of Standards (ISO) defines usability as "The extent to which a product can be used by specified users to achieve specified goals with effectiveness, efficiency, and satisfaction in a specified context of use" [2]. In order to understand the critical components of *users* and the *context of use*, the NIST usablity team visited Dulles International Airport and observed the US-VISIT operational setting.

The team identified two primary users. The first is the Customs and Border Protection (CBP) Officer, the second is the traveller entering the US. We identified four components to the interaction between the officer and the traveller in the primary entry process.

1. passport and visa inspection,
2. interview questions and answers,
3. biometrics capture (fingerprint and face), and
4. processing of various paperwork.

We observed that the language barrier can be significant. During the four hour observation period the queue of travellers was constant and the officers were processing travellers as quickly as possible.

A representative entry lane is shown in Figure 2. The lane that we observed is approximately 208 cm (6 feet 10 inches) long. The counter height on the passenger side of the lane is 124.5 cm (49 inches). The desk or processing height for the officer is 106.7 cm (42 inches). The counter width for the passenger is 22.9 cm (9 inches) and for the officer is 55.9 cm (22 inches). The aisles are not a uniform width some are 76.2 cm (30 inches), some are 91.4 cm (36 inches), and one (accessible) aisle is 152.4 cm (60 inches). The fingerprint scanner is mounted on the 124.5 cm (49 inch) counter. A Webcam, Logitech 4000 camera, is mounted on a goose neck arm on the side of the computer monitor. In the configuration we observed, the computer monitor is positioned to the side of the officer as they faced the traveller.

Figure 2. Representative Border Entry Lane

We found that passengers lined up in front of the fingerprint scanner and not the camera. Generally, the officers repositioned the webcam for every passenger to accommodate the traveller's height and position in the lane. Although some officers rarely reposition the camera since positioning the camera can be trying. We observed that positioning the webcam on the traveller while verifying the image on the computer monitor and keeping an eye on the traveller required the officer's peripheral vision which contributed to the officer's difficulty in capturing acceptable images. This activity distracts the officer from directly observing the traveler during that time, thus decreasing his/her ability to observe mannerisms and behavior -- a key element in an officer's determination as to whether a person might need to be sent for secondary inspection.

Many travellers did not know the webcam was a camera. In fact several thought it was an iris scanner and moved in too close toward the camera trying to center one eye. Travellers received no indication from the device (such as a click or shutter sound) that the picture was being taken. Finally the images were taken in landscape rather than portrait mode.

From these observations of the users and context of use the usability team identified the following human factors enhancements:

To assist the passenger the camera should:

1.   resemble a more traditional camera
2.   provide some feedback that the picture is being taken.

To assist the officer:

1.   Position the computer monitor so the officer can easily adjust the camera, see the image on the screen and see the traveler without using peripheral vision.
2.   Use the camera in portrait mode

To assist both the officer and the traveler:

1.   Provide some marking on the floor (such as footprints) to indicate to the traveler where to stand. This also assists the officer because one of the variables, the distance from the camera, is now constant. This reduces the camera adjustments for the officer, the only camera adjustment required is to accommodate the traveler's height.

From these usability observations the NIST team designed a usability experiment to examine if addressing these factors can improve face capture for US-VISIT operations.

3. METHOD

3.1. Participants

The participants were 300 adults recruited from a pool of 10,000 people who had previously agreed to participate in usability tests. There were 151 women and 149 men ranging in ages from 18 to over 65 years.

The participants ranged in self-reported height from 56 inches (142 cm) to 79 inches (201 cm). The heights were fairly normally distributed with an average height of 70.2 inches (178.3 cm) for males and 64.4 inches (163.6) for females. According to the Centers for Disease Control and Prevention (CDC) the mean individual height of men is 69 inches (175 cm) and the mean individual height of women is 63 inches (160 cm) in the US [3]. The height data collected is within 2 % of the mean in the US general population. According to the World Health Organization the worldwide mean individual male height is 5 feet 8 inches (173 cm) and the female height is 5 feet 2 inches (158 cm).

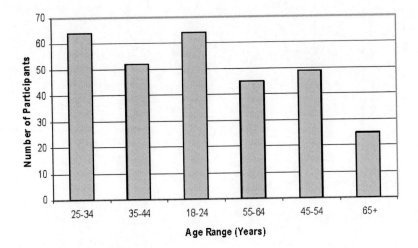

Figure 3. Participant Age Range

3.2. Equipment

This study utilized the MBARK [4] software package for controlled capture of images from a given participant. MBARK was configured to take a single, high-resolution (1944 X 2592 pixels) image. The digital camera was mounted in a "portrait" orientation to best match the aspect ratio of the human head. The tripod was physically configured so that the MBARK system operator needed only to tilt (pitch) the camera to fill the image frame. The camera was also configured to emit a "shutter" sound upon capture.

The physical layout of the face capture station is illustrated in Figure 4. Note that the goal of using seated participants was to significantly reduced the overall image capture space. A similar reduction could be accomplished by asking participants to stand on a mark on the floor. The operators were standing and could easily observe the participant, position the camera, and view the computer monitor all at once. A live viewfinder on the rear of the camera also facilitated this multitasking.

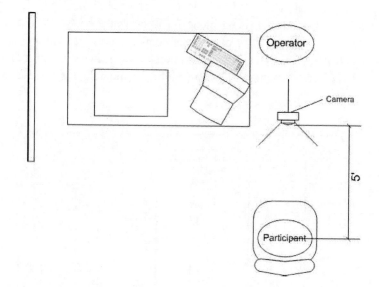

Figure 4. Face Image Capture Layout

3.3. Procedure

Each participant completed three tasks. First participants were asked to provide fingerprint images [5]. The second task was capturing a facial image. The final task for participants was an iris scan. This paper will only address face capture. After the fingerprinting tasks, the participants were asked to sit in a chair directly facing the camera to have a picture taken. The high end digital point-and shoot camera clicked similar to a traditional single lens reflex (SLR) camera's shutter when the picture was taken.

As in the operational environment the operators were given little guidance on capturing an appropriate quality face image. The only guidance was provided in the MBARK User's Manual developed for the study. Operators were asked to position the participant in front of the camera in the chair. Participants were asked to look at the camera. Throughout the capture process the operator was afforded a continuous live preview of the cameras output. Once the participant was positioned and the camera adjusted, the operator clicked a *"Capture Now"* button to capture the image. A dialog appeared displaying a thumbnail preview of resolution sufficient for a coarse examination of the captured data. If the image was acceptable the operator clicked "Accept" otherwise he clicked "Reject", repositioned the camera and/or the subject and performed a second data capture.

4. RESULTS

4.1. Face Image Quality

We based the analysis for assessing the quality of the face images on the attributes identified in ANSI INCITS 385-2004 [6] and ISO/IEC 19794-5:2005(E) [7]. Those attributes are listed in Table 1. Since there are no available fully automated conformance tests based on these standards, the approach used to evaluate the quality of the images was visual inspection to rate the first 14 attributes on a five-point scale where a value of one is least conducive to automatic face recognition and five is most conducive. The remaining six attributes are binary and were assigned values of 1 or 5, where 1 indicated the presence of the characteristic and 5 the absence.

Table 1. Face Image Attributes

Attribute	Scoring
Pose	1 to 5
Expression	1 to 5
Shoulders	1 to 5
Background	1 to 5
Subject and scene lighting	1 to 5
Shadows over the face	1 to 5
Shadows in eye-sockets	1 to 5
Hot spots	1 to 5
Eye glasses	1 to 5
Horizontal Face	1 to 5
Vertical Face Position	1 to 5
Width of head	1 to 5
Length of head	1 to 5
Obstruction*	1 to 5
Eye Color	1: undefined or 5: Color
Hair Color	1: undefined or 5: Color
Assistance in Position	1: Yes or 5: No
Eye patches	1: Yes or 5: No
Facial hairs	1: Yes or 5: No
Radical Lens Distortion	1: Yes or 5: No

As described in [8] inspecting the images manually is reliable. A human observer is capable of identifying a particular problem even in the presence of other problems, and can distinguish between failure modes. Consider an image where the facial region is saturated and also cropped at the left eye, an automated quality assessment tool may not find the face at all and report nothing. A drawback of the approach is that it is subjective. Thus, when categorizing an attribute such as saturation, there is an inherent judgment to be made. Thus, for consistency, all images were analyzed by the same individual.

4.1.1. Assessing the Quality of an Image

To illustrate the approach used to analyze the face images consider Figure 5 and each individual attribute identified in Table 1. The binary attributes were assigned a 1 or a 5 as indicated in Table 1. Consider the six binary attributes of the image in Figure 5.

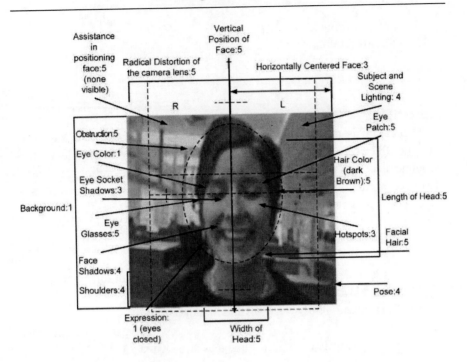

Figure 5. Face Picture Attributes

1. eye color was indeterminable and therefore was assigned a 1.
2. hair color was identifiable, assigned a 5
3. there was no facial hair, assigned a 5
4. no eye patches, assigned a 5
5. no obvious assistance in positioning, assigned a 5
6. no radical lens distortion, assigned a 5.

A 5-point scale was used to assess the remaining 14 attributes as described in the following sections.

Obstruction

The standard specifies that there shall be no head gear except in the case of religion, and in such cases, the head gear shall not cause any shadow to be cast over the face. The scale was defined as:

1. Some form of head gear;
2. Sun glasses on top of head or head band;
3. Eye glasses on top of head;

4. Large earrings;
5. No obstructions.

Using this scale the image in Figure 5 was assigned a 5.

Expression

Expression is an attribute of the full-face frontal pose that is known to strongly affect the performance of automated face recognition systems. It is recommended that the expression should be neutral (non-smiling) with both eyes open normally (i.e., not wide-open), and mouth closed, and a smile with closed jaw is not recommended. The scale was defined as

1. Eyes closed;
2. Eyes looking away from camera and/or squinting;
3. Smile where mouth opened and teeth expose but not full frontal;
4. Closed jaw smile; and
5. Neutral with both eyes open and mouth closed.

Since the eyes were closed, this image was assigned a 1.

Subject and Scene Lighting

The standard indicates that lighting shall be equally distributed on the face. There shall be no significant direction of the light from the point of view of the photographer. The scale was defined as :

1. Excessive shadows caused by head gear
2. Excessive shadows caused by poor lighting;
3. Few shadows;
4. Lighting is fairly equally distributed;
5. Lighting is distributed equally.

The lighting is fairly equally distributed in Figure 5; the image was assigned a 4.

Shadows over the Face

The standard specifies that the region of the face from the crown of the head to the base of the chin and from ear-to-ear shall be clearly visible and free of shadows. Special care should be exercised in cases when veils, scarves or headdresses cannot be removed for religious reasons to ensure these

coverings do not obscure any facial features and do not generate shadow. In all other cases head coverings shall be absent. In light of the standard specifications the following scale was developed:

1. Excessive shadows caused by head gear;
2. Large areas of shadows by poor lighting;
3. Few shadows;
4. Shadows only in eye-sockets; and
5. No shadows.

There were shadows only in the eye-sockets resulting in a score of 4.

Shadows in Eye-Sockets

The standard specifies that there shall be no dark shadows in the eye-sockets due to brow. The iris and pupil of the eyes shall be clearly visible. Our grading scale looked at the degree of shadows in the eye-sockets where we defined:

1. Shadows in both eye-sockets (caused by head gear);
2. Shadows in both eye-sockets (caused by poor sighting);
3. Shadows in only one eye socket;
4. Little shadow; and
5. No shadows.

Since there are shadows in only one eye-socket the image received a 3.

Hot Spots

It is specified in the standard that care shall be taken to avoid "hot spots" (bright areas of light shining on the face). The use of a single bare "point" light source is not acceptable. The scale was:

1. Extensive glaring from hot spots;
2. Multiple areas of hot spots (3 or more);
3. One or two hot spots;
4. One softly lighted hot spot; and
5. No hot spots.

This image was assigned a 3.

Eye Glasses

The standard specifies that eye glasses should be worn only if the individual normally wears them, and in these cases, care shall be taken that the glasses frames do not obscure the eyes. The glasses shall be clear glass and transparent so the eye pupils and irises are clearly visible. Heavily tinted glasses or sunglasses are acceptable only for medical reasons. And, there shall be no lighting artifacts or flash reflections on glasses. Using these guidelines the following scale was defined:

1. Extensive glare in both lenses;
2. Extensive glare in one lens;
3. Glare from lenses and shadows from rims;
4. Small amount of glare;
5. No glasses.

Since the person had no glasses, the image received a 5.

Background

The first step in the computer face recognition process is the segmentation of the face from the background for the purpose of registration (landmark determination). The standard recommends that the background should be plain, and shall contain no texture containing lines or curves that could cause computer face finding algorithms to become confused. Therefore, the background should be a uniform color or a single color pattern with gradual changes from light to dark luminosity in a single direction. The scale included

1. Many visible objects in background;
2. Three objects in background;
3. Two objects in background:
4. One object in background; or
5. Uniformity with no objects in background.

This image has at least 2 images in the background and was assigned a 1.

4.1.2. Face Overlay

In order to assist in evaluating the additional attributes a face overlay was developed (Figure 6). The overlay was scaled to match the size of the images on the screen. The oval shape, vertical, and horizontal lines when placed over a face image assist in the visual inspection of the geometric attributes of a face

image. The overlay is not visible in the captured images. According to the ANSI INCITS 385-2004 Standard [6], the approximate horizontal midpoints of the mouth and of the bridge of the nose shall lie on an imaginary vertical line AA at the horizontal center of the image. The upper tick-mark represents the height of the crown of the head and the distance from the edge of the picture. The lower tick-mark represents the base of the shoulder-line to the bottom edge of the picture. Line BB represents the imaginary horizontal line passing through the center of both eyes of an individual's face image. Line CC helps to line-up the horizontal midpoint of the bridge of the nose with the horizontal center of the image. The tick-marks on line CC helps with grading the horizontal midpoint between the ear lobe and the outer edge of the image. The R and L represent the right and left from the vantage point of the individual in the image looking at the camera. The oval helps with centering the face. Figure 6 illustrates the use of the face overlay. The face overlay was used to assess the following six attributes.

Pose

The pose is known to strongly affect the performance of automated face recognition systems. The standard specifications for the full-face frontal pose were used to guide the quality assessments in this study. The standard requires that the entire head is in the image, as well as the outline of the shoulders. Also, the rotation of the head shall be less than +/- 5 degrees (i.e., roll, pitch and yaw should be close to the coordinates (0,0,0). The five grading points incorporate this guidance:

1. Wearing head gear, top of head chopped off;
2. Chopped off of a shoulder;
3. Head turned at angle;
4. Full frontal not centered and;
5. Full frontal centered.

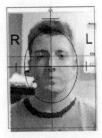

Figure 6. Example of using the face overlay (image altered for privacy)

Since the face was full frontal but not fully centered, the example in Figure 5 was given a score of 4.

Shoulders

According to the standard, the shoulders in a full-face frontal pose shall be "square on" to the camera. In our assessments, the outline of both shoulders was required to determine the squareness of the individual's shoulders. Thus, the grading scale of the shoulders was based on the available outline of both of the individual's shoulders in an image. The scale was defined as:

1. Excessive chopping of shoulder;
2. Not enough of shoulders visible;
3. Square shoulders but uneven chopping of shoulders;
4. Square shoulders, almost even chopping of shoulders; and
5. Square shoulders, even chopping of shoulders.

The shoulders were square and almost even, resulting in a score of 4.

Horizontally Centered Face

The standard specifies that the approximate horizontal midpoints of the mouth and of the bridge of the nose shall lie on an imaginary vertical line positioned at the horizontal center of the image. In our experience of assessing the images, we found that severe chopping of the image on either the individual's right or left prevented an image from being horizontally centered. The scale was defined as:

1. Severe chopping of image or excess amount of space on one side;
2. Larger amount of space on one side than the other;
3. Small difference in the spacing of the 2 sides;
4. Very small difference in the spacing; and
5. Perfect centering.

The example in Figure 5 was graded a 3.

Vertical Position of Face

The standard specifies that the face shall be positioned such that the distance between the imaginary horizontal line passing through the center of the eyes and the bottom edge of the image is 50 % to 70 % of the total vertical length of the image. The scale was defined as:

1. Large amount of head tilting and looking away from camera;
2. A large amount of head tilting;
3. Small amount of tilting eyes are off the horizontal;
4. Small amount of tilting, eyes are slightly off horizontal; and
5. Eyes are perfectly horizontal.

This image was graded as 5.

Width of Head

The standard specifies that the width of a head is the horizontal distance between the midpoints of two imaginary vertical lines drawn between the upper and lower lobes of each ear and shall be positioned where the external ear connects the head. The scale was defined as:

1. Part of the head is chopped off;
2. image is chopped too closed to the head;
3. part of the hair is chopped off;
4. the head is turned slightly causing an ear to be out of sight; and
5. Adequate head width.

The example was assigned a 5.

Length of Head

The standard specifies that the length of a head is defined as the vertical distance between the base of the chin and the crown (top of the hair). The crown to the chin portion of the Full Frontal Image pose shall be no more than 80 % of the vertical length of the image. The scale was defined as:

1. Head gear or the chopping off of the top of the head;
2. Image is chopped very close to top of the head;
3. Sunglasses on top of head ;
4. Too much head length ;
5. Adequate head length.

Using this scale the example was assessed as a 5.

4.1.3. Overall Quality

Due to hardware and software failures during the data collection process, data for several participants was found to be corrupt. Face images were

available for 267 of the 300 participants. The following tables show the counts and percentages for each of the attributes described in the previous sections.

Tables 2, 3 and 4 identify the counts and percentages of the 267 images for the binary attributes. Note that a participant may have multiple attributes in Table 2.

Tables 5 and 6 provide the number of images for each element of the rating scale for the attributes. Table 5 includes the attributes that were rated using the face overlay. Table 6 includes the remainder of the attributes.

4.1.4. Application of Selected Computational Conformance Metrics

Several of the subjective visual assessments were found to be procedurally consistent with some of the computational face conformance testing metrics [9] developed recently at NIST.

In several cases it is possible to cross-validate the two forms of quality assessment by comparing the 5-point ratings with the numerical scores of the objective measures to the extent that the measurements apply to specific image attributes.

Table 2. Binary Attributes

Attribute	Count	Percentage
Eye Patches	0	0.00%
Facial Hair	84	31.00 %
Radical distortion of the camera lens	2	0.75 %
Obstruction	19	7.00 %

Table 3. Counts of Eye Color

Eye Color	Count	Percentage
Indeterminate	35	13.00 %
Black	47	18.00 %
Blue	49	18.00%
Brown	50	19.00 %
Dark Brown	73	27.00 %
Dark Green	1	0.40 %
Gray	1	0.40%
Green	11	4.00 %

Table 4. Counts of hair color

Hair Color	Count	Percentage
Indeterminate	18	7.00 %
Brown	68	25.00 %
Dark Brown	89	33.00 %
Graying Brown	10	4.00%
Graying Dark Brown	6	2.00 %
Blond	21	8.00 %
Gray Blond	4	1.00 %
Black	36	13.00 %
Black with reddish coloring	3	1.00 %
Graying Black	4	1.00 %
Gray	3	1.00%
Red	3	1.00%
Light Brown	2	0.70%

Table 5. Face Image Data Summary

Rating	Background		Pose		Shoulders		Horizontally Centered		Vertical Position		Width of Head		Length of Head	
	Count	Percentage	Count	Percentage	Count	Percentage	Count	Percentage	Count	Percentage	Count	Percentage	Count	Percentage
1	2	75.00	32	12.00	28	10.50	2	0.75	0	0.00	9	3.37	28	10.49
2	158	59.00	31	11.60	3	1.00	18	6.74	3	1.12	7	2.62	13	4.87
3	77	29.00	38	14.00	149	56.00	184	68.91	75	28.09	9	3.37	8	3.00
4	30	11.00	162	60.70	11	4.00	23	8.61	61	22.85	7	2.62	0	0.00
5	0	0	4	1.50	76	28.46	40	14.98	128	47.94	235	88.01	218	81.65

Table 6. Face Image Data Summary

Rating	Expression		Subject/Scene Lighting		Shadows/Face		Shadows/Eyes		Hot Spots		Glasses		Obstruction	
	Count	Percentage	Count	Percentage	Count	Percentage	Count	Percentage	Count	Percentage	Count	Percentage	Count	Percentage
1	0	0.00	3	1.00	5	1.87	8	3.00	0	0.00	0	0.00	11	4.12
2	2	0.70	259	97.00	252	94.38	52	19.48	56	20.97	0	0.00	6	2.75
3	37	14.00	4	1.49	8	3.00	154	57.68	147	55.06	28	10.49	1	0.37
4	82	31.00	1	0.51	1	0.37	40	14.98	58	21.72	39	14.61	0	0.00
5	146	55.00	0	0.00	1	0.37	13	4.87	6	2.25	200	74.91	249	93.26

The majority of the computational metrics of face image quality are applied to a rectangular *face region of interest* (ROI) sampled from the full-frame image. Details of the extraction of the face ROI are described in another NIST publication currently in preparation. For the present purposes it may suffice that the vertical and horizontal limits of the sampling window are defined in relation to the image coordinates of the eyes (Appendix A:). Thus, in order to implement the computational metrics, the eye coordinates were extracted using an interactive graphics tool enabling the sampling of the eye positions as specified in the face standards.

As described previously, subjective ratings are assigned to images for assessments of both shadows and hot-spots. For purposes of computational analysis of these image defects, it is possible to consider both of these defects in terms of information loss from the image rendering, suggesting the use of an entropy measure. For gray scale images, entropy translates directly to the number of bits used in the image rendering. Its calculation shown in Appendix A: is a function of the number of gray levels used in the rendering. Thus, the typical grayscale image consisting of values 0 to 255, or 256 discrete levels of gray. Assuming the image contains at least 1 pixel at each of the 256 levels, the number of bits required would be 8, i.e., $256 = 2^8$.

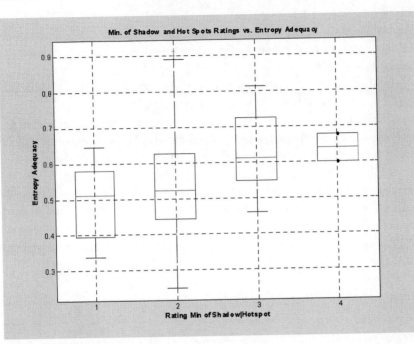

Figure 7. Distribution of entropy adequacy values for minimum ratings of shadow and hot-spots. No images have rating 5 for both shadows and hot-spots, hence only 4 rating values are used

As a measure of overall exposure of the face region, one may look simply at the entropy, or use of the available grayscale as an indicator. In order to assess shadows and hotspots, which may be more locally placed, we might define a metric that evaluates entropy on a more local scale. Such a metric, referred to as *entropy adequacy*, has been defined so as to evaluate the entropy at each position of a moving window covering the face ROI. Currently the dimension of the square window is $1/20^{th}$ of the width of the face ROI. The entropy adequacy is computed as the proportion of window positions of the total having entropy values of at least 50 % of the maximum entropy possible for the number of pixels contained in the sample window.

As entropy adequacy makes no distinction between shadows and hotspots, comparison was made between entropy adequacy and the minimum of the ratings assigned the images for shadows and hotspots. Figure 7 shows the distributions of entropy adequacy for rating values 1 to 4. Note that there were no cases in which a rating of 5 occurred for both shadows and hotspots. Moreover, the absence of whiskers for the distribution box of rating 4

indicates that only a few cases had minimum rating of 4 for both shadows and hotspots. Regardless, however, the trend of the subjective ratings is consistent with increasing entropy adequacy for reduced prominence of either shadows or hotspots.

Another of the subjective measures having corresponding computational metrics is the evaluation of eye socket shadowing. The NIST suite of computational quality metrics includes entropy measurements of rectangular regions just containing the eyes. In general the detail present in the eye regions should yield relatively high entropy values unless shadowed or the gray levels reduced by eyes being closed or by specular reflection from eyeglasses. Inasmuch as the eye shadow rating does not differentiate between right or left locations of shadows, we might compare the ratings to the minimum of the entropy calculations for the left and right eye. This comparison is shown in Figure 8 and suggests strong agreement between the subjective assessment of eye shadowing and the eye entropy metric.

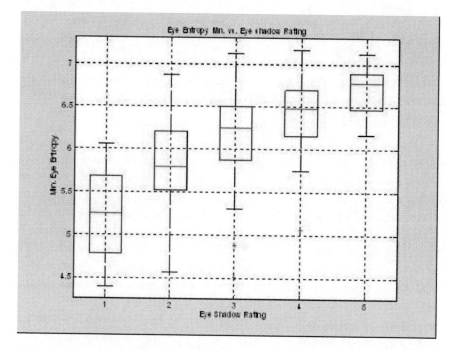

Figure 8. Distributions of minimum of eye entropy values for each of 5 rating classes of eye shadow

The subjective evaluation of face position was consistent with the description of the standard regarding vertical and horizontal placement of the head in the image frame, but differed from the computational approach. The subjective measurements examined the head position with regard to horizontal displacement from the ideal as indicated by equality of right – to – left margins from the vertical line passing through the interpupillary midpoint. Vertical placement ideal was defined as having the horizontal line passing through the eye coordinates at between 50 % to 70 % from the bottom of the image frame.

By contrast, the computational approach described head position displacement as a distance of the interpupillary midpoint from the ideal position, without consideration of whether the displacement was vertical, horizontal, or some combination. While the measurements are not strictly comparable, Figure 9 suggests some degree of consistency between the rating measure of horizontal face displacement and the computational displacement measure, at least for the rating values 2 – 5. The distribution of displacement distances for rating level 1 is degenerate, consisting of only a few values.

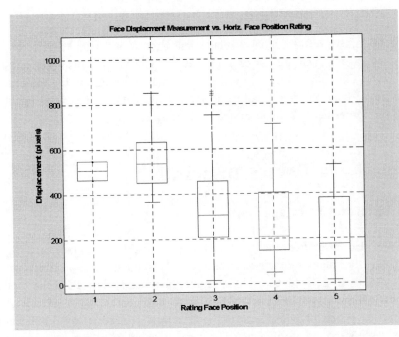

Figure 9. Computational face displacement (distance from reference position) vs. ratings of horizontal position

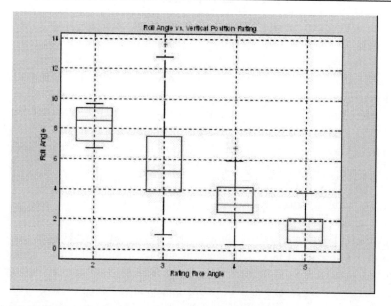

Figure 10. Roll angle measurement and ratings of vertical position

What is somewhat surprising is the apparent correlation between the subjective measure of vertical displacement and the roll angle metric. Figure 10 shows a rather strong correspondence between vertical displacement and roll angle. The rather strong agreement is explained in examining the criteria used for vertical placement rating. In making the rating for vertical position, head tilt figures heavily in the subjective assessment.

5. DISCUSSION

5.1. Efficiency of Image Capture

We also examined the time required to capture the face images or efficiency. For many biometric capture processes, the measure of efficiency is unexpectedly ill-defined. Consider a requirement that specifies that the capture process will be less than 15 seconds. This requirement does not specify when the process starts or ends. Measuring task time requires precise and easily measurable start and stop events. For many modalities, it can be difficult to establish a definitive, yet common event that delimits the task. For example, what defines the start of a face photo?

It is necessary to identify the sequential steps that are performed in order to capture a face image. As such efficiency depends on more than just the camera shutter speed, one must also take into account the arrival and departure times of the different individuals. For this study, the arrival time included both the time for the photographer to provide instructions and the time required for the individual to sit. As individuals entered, they were instructed where to sit. After sitting down, there was an occasional verbal exchange between the individual and the photographer about their pose. In addition there may have been adjustments to the camera, or repositioning of the individual, and finally the actual taking of the photograph or image capture. Thus, the definitive start and stop events that everyone performed were the subject sitting down and the image capture.

Figure 11 shows the time required to capture the face images. The median time was 12s se with an average time of 15s.

The trend of the total process time is similar to the trend that has been found in the collections of data for large-scale biometric systems as illustrated in Figure 12.

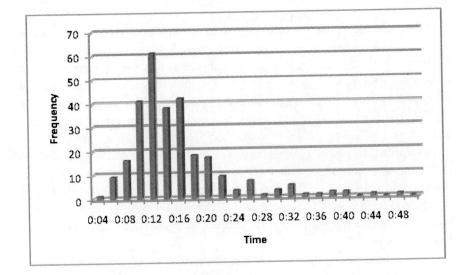

Figure 11. Total time (min:sec) to capture face

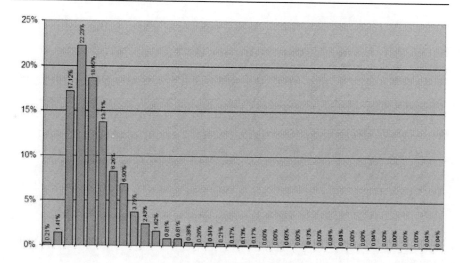

Figure 12. Timing trend of large-scale biometric system data

5.2. Quality Assessment

This usability study was designed to determine if addressing human factors could improve the current face image capture process for CBP operators without introducing additional tasks for the operators. Since operators currently use visual inspection and their judgment to determine the acceptability of the image, we developed a systematic methodology based on a similar, but highly regimented, visual inspection method for evaluating the attributes of the image quality from the ANSI [6] and ISO [7] standards.

According to a more systematic survey of the 2004 POE images described in [8] three specific defects that are easily detected using manual inspection are know to exist in the POE images: cropped faces, over-exposed faces, and non-frontal head poses. Eleven percent of the images were cropped primarily due to the camera not pointing at the subject, or the subject standing too close to the camera.

Using the methodology described in this report to evaluate the data we did not observe significant pose problems. All (100 %) of the images captured a participant's face in contrast to the US-VISIT collection. In addition, all of the participants were facing the camera. This is a significant improvement to the process currently used at the ports of entry. To further evaluate the attributes characterizing the pose and positioning of the images, we developed a face overlay template. Using this overlay we found that the majority of the images

were centered and had an appropriate pose as illustrated in Figure 13. Six attributes contribute to the poor geometry of the facial images collected by US-VISIT. Those attributes include pose, shoulders, horizontally centered, vertical position, width of head, and length of head. Figure 13 provides an overview of our attributes which contribute to pose.

Grother and Quinn [8] also applied a commercial image quality analysis tool to the 2004 POE data and found that:

- Yaw had large variance; about half the faces had more than 5 degrees of yaw.
- Eye distances were very small; the median eye distance was only about 50 pixels.
- The background was very cluttered in most of the images and frequently included partially visible faces of other people waiting in line.
- Faces were poorly centered or un-centered – generally the result of the camera operator not correctly pointing the camera at the individual.
- Many of the images were blurry, possibly due to the face or camera moving at the time of capture.

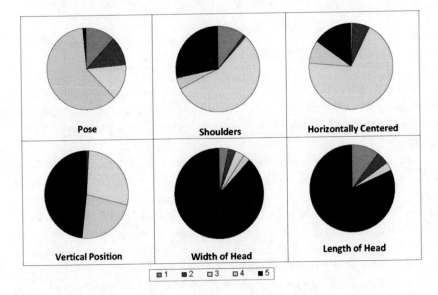

Figure 13. Attributes that contribute to poor geometry (where 1 is poor and 5 is good)

Again, applying the usability enhancements and the inspection methodology we did not observe these problems in our image data. As illustrated in Figure 13, the faces were generally centered with little variance in yaw. Eye distances were in the 210 to 575 pixel range. None of the images had any significant blurriness.

6. CONCLUSIONS AND FUTURE WORK

Currently US-VISIT Customs and Border Patrol Officers have little guidance on face image quality and use visual inspection to determine the acceptability of the image. Moreover, officers must process passengers quickly and face long queues of passengers. In this study we examined five usability and human factors enhancements to the current collection process:

1. the camera resembled a traditional camera;
2. the camera clicked as the picture was taken providing participants feedback on the process;
3. the camera was used in portrait mode;
4. the operator was facing the participant and the monitor while positioning the camera.;
5. the participants were seated at a fixed distance from the camera limiting the camera adjustments required by the operator.

Since a goal of US-VISIT is to reduce the operators workload, these enhancements were designed to have minimum impact on the operators. We specifically did not introduce any new technology or requirements on the operator.

The enhancements were designed to address the extreme conditions or departures in the captured images. For example, we found that implementing these enhancements resulted in 100 % of the images capturing a participant's face in contrast to the current US-VISIT collection and all of the participants were facing the camera with an appropriate pose (centered) and no observed distortion or blurriness. This is a significant improvement to the process currently used at the ports of entry. Thus the recommended enhancements improved the overall captured images and can be implemented easily and with little cost.

However, additional improvement may be realized by using the face overlay guide proactively. By incorporating the overlay into the workstations the officers could use the guide to center the camera on the participant's face. A follow-up study incorporating the overlay into the operators' workflow is underway.

7. REFERENCES

[1]   Nadel, L. (2007). "Approaches to Face Image Capture at US-VISIT Ports of Entry," *NIST Biometric Quality Workshop II*, Nov., retrieved from   http://www.itl.nist.gov/iad/894.03/quality/workshop07/presentations.html .

[2]   International Organization for Standards. *ISO 9241-11 Ergonomic requirements for office work with visual display terminals (VDTs) - Part 11: guidance on usability* Geneva, Switzerland: Author, (1998).

[3]   Ogden, CL; Fryar, CD; Carroll, MD; & Flegal, KM. (2004). "Mean Body Weight, Height, and Body Mass Index, United States 1960 – 2002" [Electronic Version]. *Advanced Data From Vital and Health Statistics*, *347*, Oct. Retrieved from http: // www. cdc. gov/ nchs/ data/ ad/ ad347.pdf

[4]   National Institute of Standards and Technology. *Multimodal Biometric Application Resource Kit.* Gaithersburg, MD. Retrieved from http://www.itl.nist.gov/iad/894.03/nigos/mbark.html

[5]   Theofanos, MF; Stanton, BC; Orandi, S; Micheals, R; & Zhang, NF. (2006). *Usability Testing of Ten-Print Fingerprint Capture* (*NIST IR 7403*), retrieved from http://zing.ncsl.nist.gov/biousa/

[6]   ANSI INCITS 385-2004, Face Recognition Format for Data Interchange.American National Standards Institute, Inc.

[7]   ISO/IEC 19794-5:2005(E) *Information Technology - Biometric Data Interchange Formats - Part 5: Face image data.* JTC1 : SC37, International Standard Edition, 2005. http://isotc.iso.org/isotcportal.

[8]   Grother P. & Quinn, G. (2008). *"Baseline Quality of US VISIT POE Facial Images"*, NIST Deliverable to DHS US-VISIT Face Image Quality Improvement Project, April 20.

[9]   Libert, J. *"NIST Facial Image Conformance Testing Guidelines"*, in progress.

APPENDIX A: SELECTED COMPUTATIONAL FACE IMAGE METRICS

Exposure Features

> **excerpt from ISO/IEC 19794-5:2005(E))**
> **7.4.2.1 Greyscale density**
>
> The dynamic range of the image should have at least 7 bits of intensity variation (span a range of at least 128 unique values) in the facial region of the image. The facial region is defined as the region from crown to chin and from the left ear to the right ear. This recommendation may require camera, video digitizer, or scanner settings to be changed on an individual basis when the skin tone is excessively lighter or darker than the average (preset) population.

Standards for face image data [0,0] specify several attributes which bear upon the exposure of the digital face image. These include the greyscale density of the image, i.e., the degree to which the image has used the available greyscale, 0 – 255 in an 8-bit/pixel image, the existence of shadows (under-exposure) or "hot spots" (over-exposure) in the image, and shadows in the eye regions of the image. The approach taken by NIST researcher, Libert [0] is to address each of these quality defects in terms of information loss with respect to the ideally exposed face rendering. Hence, it is appropriate to examine the information content of the image via measurements of entropy.

Entropy

First, color images are converted to greyscale (luminance) as a weighted average of the three color channels [0]

$$I_{greyscale} = 0.2989 I_{red} + 0.5870 I_{green} + 0.1140 I_{blue} \qquad (1)$$

Then entropy [0] of the greyscale image may be calculated according to the expression

$$H = -\sum_{i=1}^{n} p_i \log_2 p_i, \quad i = 1...256; \quad p_i > 0$$

(2)

where p_i = proportion of pixels in i^{th} bin of the histogram of the image region of interest (ROI) under examination.

In a typical quality evaluation, the entropy measurement is applied to a rectangular subset of the image that includes most of the face. This ROI (see Figure 144)dimension with respect to the midpoint between the eye coordinates and the measurement provides a direct assessment of the "grey-level density" of the face image. Entropy measurements are made for each of small rectangular regions containing the left right eyes

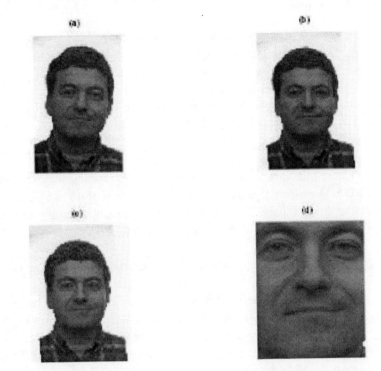

Figure 14. Frontal image from FERET image dataset. Original (a) input image (385 x 256 x3 pixels) and any non-zero roll angle removed (b). The image is converted to greyscale (c) and the face region of interest (112 x 108 pixels) cropped at boundaries set at fixed proportions of the inter-eye distance from the inter-eye midpoint (d). (Note that the example has also been transformed to the "token" format, i.e. to a standard geometry, a practice that is not used for current quality measurements.)

Entropy Adequacy of Face ROI

(excerpt from ISO/IEC 19794-5:2005(E))
7.2.8 Shadows over the face

The region of the face, from the crown (as defined in section 4.6) to the base of the chin, and from ear-toear, shall be clearly visible and free of shadows. Special care shall be taken in cases when veils, scarves or headdresses cannot be removed for religious reasons to ensure these coverings do not obscure any facial features and do not generate shadow. In all other cases head coverings shall be absent.

7.2.10 Hot spots

Care shall be taken to avoid "hot spots" (bright areas of light shining on the face). These artefacts are typically caused when one, high intensity, focused light source is used for illumination. Instead, diffused lighting, multiple balanced sources or other lighting methods shall be used. A single bare "point" light source is not acceptable for imaging. Instead, the illumination should be accomplished using other methods that meet requirements specified in this clause.

This feature attempts to detect local regions of over- or underexposure of the face ROI. The measure is defined as the proportion of n x n blocks of the face ROI that attain at least 50 % of the maximum possible entropy value for a block of a selected size. The metric is computed as follows:

1. The size of a square sample window is taken as $1/20^{th}$ of the width of the face ROI;
2. The procedure requires that the length of the window be an odd number, so if the computed length is even, it is enlarged by 1 pixel;
3. To accommodate application of the window to edges of the ROI, padding is added by symmetric mirroring of the image pixel values across the edge boundaries;
4. Centering the window on each pixel of the original face ROI, the entropy is calculated as described above and entered into an array corresponding to the dimensions of the face ROI.;
5. Given the block size, the maximum entropy possible if computed as

$$E_{max} = \frac{\log_{10} n \times m}{\log_{10} 2} = \frac{\log_{10} 81}{\log_{10} 2} = 6.3399$$

(3)

6. A count is made of the number of values in the entropy array having values greater than or equal to a threshold, $0.5E_{max}$. The count is normalized by dividing by the total number of E_{max} elements in the entropy array to form a single proportion, i.e. value between 0 and 1. A value of 1.0 would indicate that all sampled blocks attain at least 50% of the maximum entropy possible. Areas of "hot spots" or shadows as well as low contrast should yield lower values of this metric. The 50 % threshold and the size of the sample window are somewhat arbitrary at this point, supported only by a few tests. Further testing is planned, but the intent of the measure is to evaluate image exposure on a local level.

Eye Exposure

> **(excerpt from ISO/IEC 19794-5:2005(E))**
> **7.2.9 Shadows in eye-sockets**
>
> There shall be no dark shadows in the eye-sockets due to the brow. The iris and pupil of the eyes shall be clearly visible.

The following features form the beginning of analysis of exposure in eye regions. The eyes tend to be the most detailed regions of the face image and if properly exposed should have relatively high entropy values, if not the highest of any subregion of the face. Moreover, one would expect entropy values should be about equal values for both eyes unless illumination is uneven across the face.

For this measurement. A rectangular ROI is sampled about each image eye coordinate pair, sized proportional to the image width (currently $W_{roi} = 0.1 \times W_{face}$ and $H_{roi} = 0.05 \times W_{face}$, selected by inspection of images). Entropy as specified above is then computed for each eye.

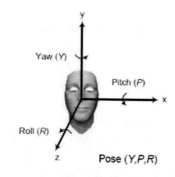

Figure 15. Depiction of pose reference axes. (from INCITS 385-2004 [0])

Pose/Geometry

Face image geometry, especially yaw and pitch orientation of the face in the image frame, may have the greatest single effect upon matcher performance. If not excessive, roll may be corrected via 2-D affine transformation, commonly applied by face matchers. Pitch and yaw are much more difficult to measure precisely much less to rectify. But unless the matcher incorporates some reasonably accurate rectification scheme able to recover a frontal face image pose from some non-frontal viewpoint, most comparison methods will be challenged. Face standards such as [0, 0]for subject (or face) pose to be described relative to three axes as shown in Figure 15 Optimum or frontal pose would have 0° departure for all three measures yaw, pitch, and roll (Y, P, R). Assuming that a matcher is able to find critical reference points such as eye coordinates, roll should be removed during the geometric normalization (or tokenization) step or in the face ROI sampling procedure as described. Non-zero yaw and pitch angles are more troublesome.

The present feature set includes measures for face position and roll (also known as in-plane rotation). Additional features developed at NIST include a set of candidate features aimed at sensing departures from the frontal, $Y = 0°$, yaw condition by measuring symmetry of the face ROI. These features are not included here as this was not evaluated in the subjective quality assessment.

Face Position

Face position is taken as the distance (in pixels) of the inter-eye midpoint from the optimal placement relative to its position in a token image as specified in ISO/IEC and INCITS face standards [0, 0]. The midpoint of actual eye positions is the mean of the eye coordinates (column, row) values. According to the standard, the appropriate vertical placement of the inter-eye midpoint is given as $0.6W$ (W = image width) from the top of the token format image in which height is specified to be $W/0.75$. The untokenized image may not conform to a standard height. Yet an "optimum" position proportional to that of the tokenized frame might be calculated using the top of the the acquired image as the reference. In this case, the position may be computed as $0.45H$, where H is the height of the acquired image. Distance between actual and optimal eye midpoint position is then computed using the distance formula

$$d_{pixels} = \sqrt{(x_1 - x_2)^2 + (y_1 - y_2)^2} \quad ,$$

(4)

where (x_1, y_1), (x_2, y_2) are coordinates of actual and optimal inter-eye midpoints respectively.

This metric does not resolve horizontal and vertical components of the displacement vector, but the additional values could be provided if the need is justified. In this case, however, it might be more appropriate to describe the displacement using conventional vector notation of a length and an angle.

Roll Angle (In-Plane Rotation)

Roll or in-plane rotation angle (in degrees) is measured with respect to offset of eye coordinates from horizontal, $R = 0°$. Here the measurement is implemented by the function *interocular.m* Roll angle is generally corrected during geometric normalization performed by the matcher. However, Grother [0] reports that mean differences of greater than 8° between probe and gallery image pairs adversely affects matcher verification performance in spite of apparent geometric transformation to 0° roll angle.

Given x, y coordinates of right and left eye, roll angle, R, can be computed via

$$R_{deg} = \tan^{-1}(\frac{y_r - y_l}{x_r - x_l}) \times \frac{180°}{\pi}$$

(5)

where (xr, yr) and (xl, yl) are right and left eye coordinates.

REFERENCES

ANSI-INCITS 385-2004 Face Recognition Format for Data Interchange. American National Standards Institute, Inc.

Gonzalez, RC; Woods, RE; & Eddins, SL. (2003). *Digital Image Processing Using MATLAB*, New Jersey, Prentice Hall.

Grother. P. (2004). Face Recognition Vendor Test 2002: Supplemental Report, NISTIR 7083, February 2.

ISO/IEC 19794-5:2005(E) Information Technology - Biometric Data Interchange Formats - Part 5: Face image data. JTC1 : SC37, international standard edition, 2005. http://isotc.iso.org/isotcportal.

J. M Libert Face Image Quality: Part 1 Algorithms [in preparation for publication as a NIST Internal Report].

Poynton, CA. (1996). A *Technical Introduction to Digital Video*, NY, John Wiley & Sons.

In: Design and Performance of Biometric System   ISBN: 978-1-60692-978-0
Editor: John T. Elsworth   © 2010 Nova Science Publishers, Inc.

Chapter 2

USABILITY AND BIOMETRICS: ENSURING SUCCESSFUL BIOMETRIC SYSTEMS

National Institute of Standards and Technology

ABSTRACT

This handbook provides an overview of the user-centered design process and examples of how the process can be applied to the design and development of biometric technology systems.

Keywords Biometrics, Usability, User-Centered Design, Requirements Analysis, User and Task Analysis, User Evaluation, Usability Testing

FORWARD

As the NIST's Information Access Division, Visualization and Usability Group began to study the usability of biometric technologies and applications we realized that our partners in the biometric community were unfamiliar with usability terminology and methodologies. Part of fostering an effective partnership is communicating the value and benefit of the usability discipline. As the visibility and interest in our usability and biometric research increased

it became clear that a handbook introducing usability would benefit the community as a whole and this document was created.

This handbook provides a common understanding and vocabulary for usability to encourage communication between usability and biometric researchers and practitioners. It begins by examining the biometric collection process and the role of the user and user characteristics. We examine the concept of usability and how it is defined. We introduce the user-centered design process and the value of the process to the development of biometrics systems. The elements of the user centered design process including context of use, user and organizational requirements, design solutions, and evaluation techniques are defined and described. Finally a list of usability methods and techniques are elaborated.

We hope that this handbook will be useful in continuing to promote a collaborate research environment between the biometric and usability research communities.

1. THE BIOMETRIC PROCESS

The Biometric View of the Process

To date, the design, development and evaluation of biometric technologies[1] has understandably been focused on system performance, functionality, reliability and precision including resolution of sampling, speed, accuracy, and error rates. In the beginning stages of development, it was necessary to focus primarily on the performance of biometric systems. As these new technologies mature, it's important to begin to evaluate other factors, including the usability of these systems.

One aspect of biometric systems that has not been traditionally considered is the user. The user brings innate qualities and experiences to the interaction that affect performance. Without a careful consideration of user qualities, biometric system designers and evaluators will struggle to make significant improvements, which advances in technology alone cannot achieve.

The biometric view of the process typically focuses solely on the technology. This view of the system and technology is presented in the illustration below.

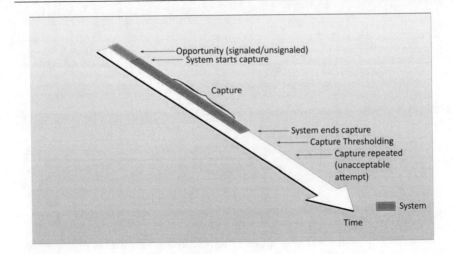

Figure 1. Biometric View of the Process.

In order to make more substantial improvements to the performance of biometric technologies, it is essential to take the user into consideration.

"We can no longer focus on one half of the problem. It is necessary to examine the human and usability. Up to this point, the user has been in some sense forgotten from the process, yet the user is key to providing the biometric sample. The user starts the process and the user's fingerprint sample determines the success of the process and the system as a whole." (Theofanos, Stanton, Michaels, & Orandi).

USER INVOLVEMENT IN THE BIOMETRIC PROCESS

Users are a key component in the biometric process, as users begin the process with a presentation and ideally end the process by submitting a high-quality, accurate sample. Their interaction with the system is essential to a holistic understanding of the biometric process.

To date, many biometric systems have focused solely on the limitations and capabilities of a technology, without truly considering the impact a user's characteristics, experience levels and abilities will have on a biometric system.

The diagram below illustrates the two-way interaction, or relationship, between the user and the system during the biometric process.

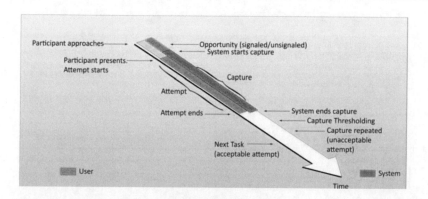

Figure 2. User Involvement in the Biometric Process.

Not only does the user play an integral role in the submission of a sample, a user's innate characteristics have a substantial impact on the ultimate success of a biometric system.

Demographic Characteristics

Innate characteristics can significantly affect a user's performance and influence the ability of the system to perform successfully. For instance, consider the impact of the following characteristics on the design of a biometric system:

- Age
- Gender
- Experience
- Ability

By designing with these characteristics in mind, developers of biometric systems can produce a system that is more effective and efficient. With a focus on users and the usability of biometric systems, design teams have the opportunity to improve image captures, increase throughput, and reduce errors.

Following is a partial list of design questions that project teams must consider in the creation of a biometric system. Please note, this list is not an exhaustive list of design considerations. Rather, it is intended to stimulate design teams to begin thinking about the needs of users and the potential impact of users' inherent qualities on the performance of a system.

Age

- How does an individual's age affect the quality of a sample?
- Does age affect users' abilities to learn and use a biometric system?
- Are younger users more successful in their attempts?
- Do older users take longer to present a sample?

Gender

- Does gender affect the quality of a sample?
- Does gender affect the accuracy of a sample?
- What role does gender play, if any, in the presentation and capture of a sample?

Experience & Ability

- What role does experience play in users' abilities to present a sample?
- Are more experienced individuals more successful?
- Do first-time users struggle more than experienced users?
- How does past experience affect a user's interaction with a system?
- How do disabilities affect the user in submitting a biometric sample?
- Which disabilities impact success in presentation and capture?

In addition to these demographic characteristics, it is also important to consider other opportunities to enhance the usability of a biometric system through the use of user-centered instructions, greater awareness of anthropometrics, enhanced affordance and improved accessibility.

To that end, we have provided some additional design questions related to these issues below:

Instructional Guides & System Feedback

- How can designers create intuitive instructional materials (posters, signs, etc.) for end users who may not speak the same language?
- How does culture impact the understanding of symbols, colors and iconography?
- What types of cultural conventions must be considered?

- What types of instructional materials are most appropriate given the location and environment in which the biometric system is located? Where should instructional guides be positioned? At what height?
- What types of feedback should a biometric system provide to end users? Audio? Visual? Sensory?
- At what point in the process should the system provide feedback? How frequently should feedback be given? What is the most effective and efficient way to provide this feedback?

Anthropometrics

As measurements used to describe the user of a product, anthropometrics provide data on average body dimensions that exist in the larger population. Gathered by taking measurements from a large number of users in a variety of positions, anthropometrics provide biometric designers with information needed to create more usable systems.

- How can designers use established standards to design the physical characteristics of a biometric system?
- How does an individual's height affect the quality of a sample?
- Does the height of a system affect the quality of samples?
- Can anthropometric data be used to inform the optimal height and position of a biometric system?
- How does hand geometry affect the size of the platen?

Affordance

First introduced into the world of human-computer interaction by Donald Norman in the book "The Design of Everyday Things" (Norman, 1988), affordance refers to the properties of an object that allow a user to perform an action. In designing systems, developers often look to create a sense of affordance so that users understand that they can interact with a product or system. With regard to biometric systems, this interaction may come in the form of a physical design (do users understand from the design of the hardware what actions they should take) or in the form of a systems' graphical

interface (does the software interface invoke users to interact with the biometric system in an appropriate manner).

While actual affordance is a key component of any given system, it is also important for designers to consider perceived affordances. For instance, do users expect an action to occur when in actuality the function doesn't exist? Understanding how users expect a system to perform is just as important as understanding how users interact with the intended affordances.

- Do users understand what to do when they encounter a biometric device or system?
- What actions do users perceive are available?
- What information does the biometric system provide to users to communicate the actions users should take?
  - For fingerprint readers, do users understand what actions they should take? Do they know where to place their finger(s)? Can they determine which finger(s) to use? Do they understand how to position and present their finger(s)? Do they know when the scan is completed?
  - For face recognition or iris/retina scanning, can users determine how to use these systems? Do they know how to position their bodies?
  - For voice recognition, do users know how to present their voice?
  - Etc...

Accessibility

Accessibility refers to the ability of all types of users to successfully access and use a biometric system, including those who are visually- or hearing-impaired, individuals who use a wheelchair, and other types of individuals who may have difficulty using a product or system that doesn't take their needs into consideration.

- How can biometric designers create systems that will be usable for individuals who are visually-impaired and may have difficulty using posted instructional guides or feedback provided through a graphical interface? What other types of cues can be provided for this user population?

- What about hearing-impaired users who may have difficulty distinguishing or understanding audio cues?
- How can biometric systems be designed to accommodate users in wheelchairs, including the height of a system and allow ample area around the technology for users to access the system?
- What other types of needs should be considered? How can designers create a biometric system that is universally accessible and usable to all audiences?

By taking into consideration a users' inherent demographic characteristics, as well as instructional guides and feedback, anthropometrics, affordance, and accessibility, biometric developers have a much greater chance of producing a truly usable, user-friendly system.

USER-CENTERED VIEW OF THE BIOMETRIC PROCESS

In its entirety, the user-centered process involves all facets of the biometric system. This holistic view involves not only the system and its response to a presentation, but also the inherent qualities of users and their interaction with the biometric system.

The diagram below integrates these essential usability components to illustrate a truly user-centered process that takes into consideration the needs and characteristics of users instead of simply regarding users as inactive participants in the process.

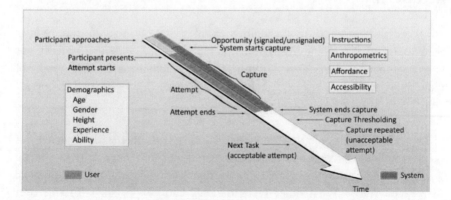

Figure 3. User View of the Biometric Process with User Attributes and Characteristics

By understanding the essential role a user plays in the biometric process and viewing the process as a two-way relationship in which the system and user are partners with the same goal in mind, we can begin to have a substantial impact on the design and usability of these systems. By coming to terms with the inherent characteristics and interactions users have with a system, design teams can make better informed decisions, thus taking some of the guesswork out of the biometric design process.

In the next sections of this handbook, we'll discuss a proven user-centered design process that will help designers and developers of biometric systems focus on the needs and characteristics of users in order to build a truly successful product.

CONCLUSION

In order to improve the usability of biometric systems, it is critical to take a holistic approach that considers the needs of users as well as the entire experience users will have with a system, including the hardware, software and instructional design of a system. Adopting a user-centric view of the biometric process is not only beneficial to the end users, but a user-centric view can also help to improve the performance and effectiveness of a system.

In order to understand the best way to improve the usability of a system, it is important to fully understand the components of a usable system. In the next chapter, we will take a closer look at the concept of usability and how it is defined.

2. WHAT IS USABILITY

Definition of Usability

At its core, user-centered design is based upon the concept of developing a usable, useful system or product. To fully understand user-centered design, it is essential to understand the features inherent in a usable system.

Usability helps to ensure that systems and products are easy to learn, effective to use and enjoyable from the user's perspective. Defined as:

"The extent to which a product can be used by specified users to achieve specified goals with effectiveness, efficiency, and satisfaction in a specified context of use." (ISO 13407:1999)

Looking closely at the definition, usability goals such as effectiveness, efficiency and satisfaction are specifically called out. Additional attributes of usability that you may also want to consider include:

- Effective to use (effectiveness)
- Efficient to use (efficiency)
- Enjoyable to use (satisfaction)
- Easy to learn (learnability)
- Easy to remember (memorability)

The table that appears on the next page lists each of these usability goals and provides a short description of each, along with a few questions for biometric system designers to consider.

When designing a usable biometric system, it is important to consider the various aspects of the user experience, including:

These usability goals can, and should, be translated into measureable usability objectives for your specific biometric product. Using these metrics, biometric designers and developers can assess a system's usability. Examples of commonly used usability criteria are:

Success rates: Can users successfully provide a high-quality sample? (*Effectiveness*)

Time on task: Can users quickly use the product? (*Efficiency*)

Time to learn a task: How long does it take a user to learn a product? (*Learnability*)

Number of errors made over time: Can users remember how to use it? (*Memorability*)

Users' satisfaction level: Are users uncomfortable using the system? (*Satisfaction*)

Specific metrics and ways to measure usability will be discussed in more detail in the chapter on Evaluation.

Usability Goals	Definition
Effectiveness	Measure of how well a user can perform a task: • Can users *successfully* provide a high-quality sample? • Can users *accurately* provide a sample?
Efficiency	Measure of how quickly a user can perform work and the error rate in doing so: • Are users able to *quickly* accomplish goals? • Can users perform tasks with *few errors*?
Satisfaction	Measure of user attitudes, perceptions, feelings and opinions regarding the system: • How well does the interface *avoid inducing user discomfort and frustration?* • Are users *intimidated* by using the biometric system?
Learnability	Measure of how rapidly a user can become productive: • Can users *learn how to use* the biometric system? • *How long* should it take a user *to learn* the interface? • Are users able to use the system (to some defined level of competence) after instruction or training?
Memorability	Measure of how well a returning user forms a mental model of the biometric system and remembers how to use it: If a user has used the system before, can he/she remember enough to use it effectively the next time or does the user have to start over again learning everything? How do experienced users differ from infrequent/novice users? • After not using the interface for a period of time, how long should it take for the user to get up to speed?

In its narrowest sense, usability involves the evaluation of a system; in its broadest sense, usability involves users throughout the requirements definition, design, development and evaluation phases of a technology to produce a system which is measurably easier to use, learn and remember.

Too often usability evaluations are carried out after a product has been designed and developed. Although, this can help to correct many of the things that should have been done right in the first place, it minimizes the impact a proven user-centered design process can have on a project. When usability evaluations are conducted at the end of a project lifecycle, recommendations and improvements are much more costly to make. By including users early on in the design lifecycle, it is possible to integrate user feedback and usability recommendations into the initial designs and draft prototypes, when it is much easier and less costly to make changes.

The importance of including users early on in the development process cannot be emphasized enough. The best and most successful systems involve users in the early stages of the design in order to continually evolve and refine the design in an iterative process.

CONCLUSION

A truly usable system takes into consideration the needs of users throughout the design, development and evaluation process. It involves:

- Analyzing the **context of use**
- Defining the **user and organizational requirements**
- Developing a **design solution** to meet those requirements
- Conducting **evaluations** to test the design against the defined requirements

The following sections of this handbook will introduce a user-centered design process that involves users throughout the product lifecycle to develop biometric systems that improve ease-of-use, reduce product complexity, enhance system performance, increase users' satisfaction, and minimize the number of errors that may occur.

3. USER-CENTERED DESIGN

Introduction to User-Centered Design

User-centered design is an approach to the design and development of a system or technology that aims to improve the ability of end users to effectively and efficiently use the product. It seeks to improve the user experience of an entire system from hardware design to software implementation, involving all aspects of a technology, including a system's byproducts, such as help documentation and training materials.

By involving users in the design, development and evaluation of a biometric system, user-centered design works to create more usable products that meet the needs of its users. This, in turn, reduces the risk that the resulting system will under-deliver or fail.

User-centered design involves (ISO 13407:1999):

- early focus on users, tasks, and environment;
- the active involvement of users;
- an appropriate allocation of function between user and system;
- the incorporation of user-derived feedback into the (biometric) system design;
- iterative design whereby a prototype is designed, tested and modified.

This process is illustrated below:

Although there is a substantial body of knowledge and research regarding user-centered design and usability principles, much of this information is not yet integrated in the standard design and development processes of today's biometrics systems.

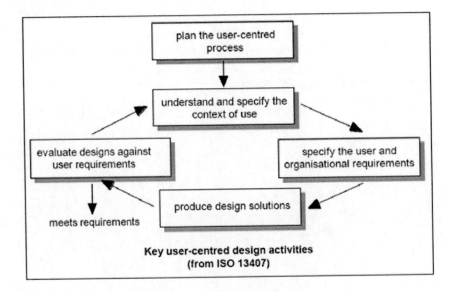

Figure 4. User-Centered Design Process (ISO 13407:1999).

User-Centered Design for Biometric Systems

This handbook will outline a user-centered design methodology for the development of biometric technologies. This process is based on the International Organization for Standardization (ISO) standard mentioned above.

The user-centered design process outlined in this handbook includes:

- Defining the **Context of Use**
  Including operational environment, user characteristics, tasks, and social environment

- Determining the **User & Organizational Requirements**
  Including business requirements, user requirements, and technical requirements

- Developing the **Design Solution**
  Including the system design, user interface, and training materials

- Conducting the **Evaluation**
  Including usability, accessibility, and conformance testing

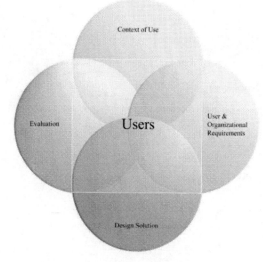

Figure 5. Biometric User-Centered Design Process

This handbook will outline each of the steps illustrated below in order to enable developers and designers of biometric systems to implement this proven process on their own projects.

The key to this iterative process is that it is **User-Centered, Research-Based, and Performance-Driven**.

User-Centered	Identifies the types of users who will be using the system, including end users, system operators, and system analysts.
	Ensures that the needs of users are considered in the design and development of the biometric device.
	Includes users' feedback through user research and evaluation.
Research-Based	Employs research to learn about users, their needs, their tasks, their environment, their level of experience, etc.
	Conducts on-going research with users of biometric devices by observing users interacting with the actual system or product and identifying areas for improvement.
Performance-Drive	Utilizes information gathered from users in the development to ensure that design decisions are data-driven.
	Elicits continual feedback from users and measures user performance to ensure that design improvements have a measureable impact on users' effectiveness, efficiency and satisfaction (ISO 13407:1999) with a biometric system.

Independent of any product design lifecycle, user-centered design works as part of other development lifecycles, including waterfall, spiral and agile models. It is an evolutionary process in which project teams design, test and continually refine a system.

By following this iterative, user-centered design process, biometric development teams can have a measurable impact on the usability and ease-of-use of their systems.

Benefits of Usability

Not only do usability improvements lead to better, easier-to-use products, they also lead to improved user performance and satisfaction as well as substantial cost savings. By designing a biometric system with usability in mind, development teams can enhance ease of use, reduce system complexity, improve user performance and satisfaction, and reduce support and training costs. Additionally, improved usability can result in a significant return on investment, including:

- Improved system performance, greater accuracy, and fewer attempts required
- Decreased time to capture an acceptable sample and increased efficiency
- Improved productivity and fewer errors
- Reduced need for assistance from system operators
- Decreased support and training costs
- Increased user acceptance

CONCLUSION

In this section, the various facets of the user-centered design lifecycle were introduced, including four main components:

- Defining the **Context of Use**
- Determining the **User & Organizational Requirements**
- Developing the **Design Solution**
- Conducting the **Evaluation**

In the next chapter, we will take a closer look at the context of use and how it is defined. The remaining chapters of this handbook will discuss each of the user-centered design phases outlined above. Additionally, a chapter on Usability Methods has also been included to describe some of the methods discussed in this handbook.

4. CONTEXT OF USE

Define Context of Use

The first stage of the user-centered design process involves defining the "context of use."

The use of all products, including biometric technologies, takes place within a context. The actual conditions under which a biometric system is used must be considered at the forefront of any project to ensure that the design of the system will meet the needs of users and the objectives of the organization once the system is implemented in a real-world environment.

Awareness of contextual factors is important throughout the development process. Context of use does not simply involve the users' context of use, it involves a much broader view of context, including the *business environment* in which the biometric system is being developed, the *operational environment* in which the system will be used, and the social environment in which the system will be implemented. For purposes of this document, we will focus mainly on the user environment and discuss the business environment more in the following chapter on User and Business Requirements.

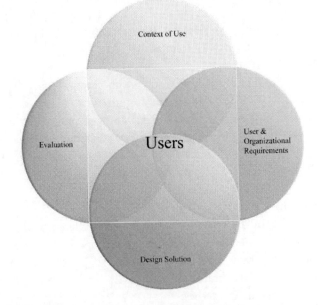

Figure 6. Context of Use within the User-Centered Design Process

To develop a usable product, the context in which the biometric system will be used should be considered from the very early stages of product design lifecycle.

Defining Your Users

The central objective of designing a usable system is to meet the needs of users within their operational context. To do this, it is imperative that users are involved throughout the biometric design process. The design of the system should:

- Focus on users' needs and expectations
- Involve users throughout
- Integrate feedback from users into the design

But before you can focus on users' needs and expectations, you must first identify who your users are. There are several different ways to categorize user groups, including:

Primary users:	End users for whom the biometric system is primarily designed.
Secondary users:	End users who interact with the biometric system, but not for its primary purpose or users who interact with the system infrequently.
	OR
Direct stakeholders:	End users who interact directly with the biometric system.
Indirect stakeholders:	Individuals who may not directly interact with the biometric system but their performance is affected by the interaction of the direct stakeholders with the system.

To begin, simply identify your audiences.

Think about all of the types of users who may interact with your system on a regular basis and then create a list of these users. If your user population contains groups of people who use the system to perform different sets of tasks, or who have considerable differences in ability or experience, then divide them into separate user types.

Next, group the users into categories, such as primary or direct stakeholders and secondary or indirect stakeholders. In doing this exercise, consider the relative importance of each group and begin to create prioritized lists of user groups.

Primary or Direct Stakeholders: **Secondary or Indirect Stakeholders**

1. End User_____	1. System Analyst_____
2. System Operator_____	2. _____
3. _____	3. _____
4. _____	4. _____
5. _____	5. _____

Once this process is complete, begin to define the role each user will have with the biometric system. See below for an example.

DEFINING USERS FOR A FINGERPRINT READER

In considering the design of a fingerprint reader, there are at least three basic types of users:

USER GROUP	ROLE
• The end user	The person who provides the fingerprint
• The system operator	The person who operates the device
• The system analyst	The person who interprets the results

The end users and the system operators are *direct* stakeholders, in that they interact directly with the fingerprint reader. The system analysts are *indirect* stakeholders, in that they may not directly interact with the system but their performance is affected by the interaction of the direct stakeholders with the biometric device.

While this analysis defines, at a high-level, the types of users who use the system (both from the front-end and the back-end perspective), it is critical to define these audiences even more. For instance, within the End User group, there may be several subgroups, such as:

- First-time users
- Younger users

OR

- Frequent users
- Older users

While this is just a beginning, the tools and resources on the following pages will help biometric teams to better define and identify their user groups.

Understanding Your Users

Once you have identified and prioritized your users, the next step is to *understand* your users, their needs, interests and goals. Start by learning everything you can about your user audiences, including:

- Demographics and physical attributes
- Knowledge level, familiarity with the product, and skills
- Users' tasks and goals
- Users' environment and context in which they interact with the system
- Social and organizational environment

User Demographics

First consider the demographic and anthropometric characteristics of your users. The following list of characteristics is a sample list of attributes to consider. As you contemplate your design, take care to include any characteristic which may influence or affect the usability of your product, including:

- Age
- Gender
- Height
- Ethnicity, Nationality, Language and Culture
- Education

- Experience and Knowledge Level
- Attributes Regarding Accessibility

DO DEMOGRAPHIC DIFFERENCES AFFECT A DESIGN?

A recent study conducted by NIST to determine if experience and habituation would impact users' behavior and success with a fingerprinting device found that factors such as age and gender had an immediate impact on users' performance. (Theofanos, Micheals, Scholtz, Morse, & May, 2006)

How Do You Define User Demographics?

- The User Demographics Table on the following page will help you identify the demographic characteristics of your users and will also be used in the next phase of the process User and Organizational Requirements to define possible user requirements.
- At this stage of the process, it is not necessary to define the user requirements, although a sample set of design questions have been provided in the following table.
- Please note, this exercise should be conducted for each group of users you identified in the previous section.

User Type: End User or Presenter

USER ENVIRONMENT

Once the user characteristics have been defined, begin to consider the context of use, including environmental factors, such as:
- When and where will users access the biometric system?
- What is the environment like?
  - Placement of device?
  - Height, angle and distance from portal?
  - Lighting?
  - Noise levels?

Table 1. User Demographics

Characteristics	Questions to Consider: Defining the Characteristics	Questions to Consider: User Requirements
Age	*What is the average age range of this user group?* *• For example: 18-75.*	*• Do older users require larger text or louder audio cues?* *• Are younger users more successful?*
Gender	*What is the gender distribution?* *• For example: 50% Male/50% Female*	*• Is one gender more successful?*
Anthropometrics	*What is the average height of the population? What is the range?*	*• How does a user's height affect his/her ability to present?* *• Does the height of the system affect users' abilities to present?* *• Can the user reach the system?*
Ethnicity Nationality, Language, Culture	*What kinds of users will access the biometric system? From which ethnicities and nationalities? Is there a common language or culture?*	*• If no common language exists, how does this impact the design of system feedback and instructional guides?*
Education	*What is the typical education level of your users?* *• For instance: Less than high school, high school diploma, college degree, advanced degree, etc.*	*• How does education affect system usage? Does the biometric system need to accommodate users with limited or no reading skills?*
Experience and Knowledge Level	*How many of the users will have experience with this system or a similar type of system? How many of the users will be new or first-time visitors? What is users' familiarity level with the biometric system? Have users had any type of training on the system?* *• For instance: Novice (Infrequent users), Intermediate (Moderate users), Advanced (Frequent users)*	*• Do the needs of first-time visitors differ from those of more frequent or regular users?*
Attributes regarding Accessibility	*Are there other characteristics that have not been considered?* *• For instance: Individuals with vision or hearing impairments, individuals who use a wheelchair, etc.*	*• How do these attributes affect the design of a biometric system? What design requirements must be considered to make the system universally accessible?*

- Temperature? Humidity?
- Placement, type and format of instructions (signs, labels, icons)?
- Assistance/Help? Will the devices be staffed or unstaffed? What types of help are available?

How Do You Define the User Environment?

- The User Environment Table on the following page will help you identify the context of use and will also be used in the next phase of the process User and Organizational Requirements to define possible user requirements.
- At this stage of the process, it is not necessary to define the user requirements, although a sample set of design questions have been provided in the following table.
- Please note, this exercise should be conducted *for each type of environment* the biometric system will be available in.

USER GOALS & TASKS

Once the user characteristics have been identified, it is time to turn your attention to conducting a user and task analysis, including answering questions such as:

- Why will these stakeholders use your system? What is the user's purpose?
- What are the needs, interests and goals of your users?
- Are users cooperative or not cooperative?
- How will users interact with the system?
- What are the key tasks a user must perform?
- Which tasks will users perform frequently?
- Which tasks are critical to a user's success with the biometric system?
- Which tasks are critical to the success of the organization?

User Environment:_____

Table 2. User Environment

Characteristics	Questions to Consider: Defining the Characteristic	Questions to Consider: Potential Effects
Location	*In what environment will the device be located?* *What are the physical characteristics of this location?* • *For example: Airport, Border Crossing, etc.*	• *How does the physical environment of this location affect or influence the design and usage of the system (i.e. Are sounds audible in an airport environment)?*
Placement of Device	*in what physical location (within in the environment) will the device be placed?* *What is the height of the device? Is there ample space for an individual in a wheelchair to maneuver?* *How will users access the device? Will there be waiting lines?* *Where is the device situated? On a desk? Table? Etc.*	• *How does the placement of the biometric device affect users' ability to use and access the system?* • *What types of spatial requirements are necessary to facilitate frequent use by a large number of users?* • *How does a user's height or the height of the system affect auser's ability to use the device?*
Temperature/ Humidity	*What the average temperature for the device location? What are the extreme temperatures? Is the area humid?*	• *How does the outside environment affect the performance of a system?* • *How does temperature and humidity affect the capture of a high-quality sample?*
Lighting	*What types of lighting are utilized?*	• *How does the level of lighting affect the*
	Will the system be utilized at night as well as during the day? • *For instance: Low light, florescent lighting, natural light (sunlight), night light, etc.*	*readability or visibility of graphical displays?*
Noise	*What is the noise level?* • *For instance: Quiet, noisy, etc.*	• *How does the noise level affect an individual's ability to hear audio cues and feedback*

Table 2. (Continued)

Characteristics	Questions to Consider: Defining the Characteristic	Questions to Consider: Potential Effects
		provided by the system?
Instructions	*Where are instructions placed? What is the format of instructions (signs, labels, icons)? Are users supposed to review instructions prior to presenting (i.e. while waiting in line)? What size are the instructions?*	• *If instructions are posted, are the icons and lettering large enough for all to see?* • *Are the instructions obstructed?* • *What is the appropriate height to place instructional guides?*
Assistance / Help	*What types of help and assistance is provided? Is the device staffed or unstaffed?*	• *Given the environment, what is the best way to present error feedback and help information?*

How Do You Define User Goals and Tasks?

- The User Tasks & Prioritization Table on the following page will help you define the tasks that users will need to perform and rate the task based on:
  - Frequency of use (*How frequently will users perform this task?*)
  - Importance (*How critical is this task to users? To the organization?*)
  - Feasibility (*How feasible is it to include this function in the design?*)
  - Vulnerability (*If this is an existing system, is there reason to believe that this task is prone to usability issues?*)
- At this stage of the process, it is not necessary to define the importance of a task to the organization, the feasibility of a task, or the vulnerability of a task to usability issues.
- During the User and Business Requirements phase, you will re-visit this table to prioritize users' tasks with regard to the organization's objectives.

- During the Design phase, you will evaluate the feasibility of each task to determine which tasks should be translated into biometric system requirements.
- During the Evaluation phase, you will consider the vulnerability of a task to usability issues. Tasks that are susceptible to usability issues and are also important to users and the organization should be at the top of the list of things to evaluate.
- Please note, this exercise should be conducted *for each group of users* you identified in the previous section.

Once these high-level tasks have been defined, development teams should break each task down into its subcomponents. Many teams find that the development of use cases can be a particularly effective way to document this step-by-step process. Use cases are used by many software development teams to document the way a user interacts with a system, under various conditions. A use case is usually a text document (but it can be in the form of a process diagram) that describes the steps a user takes to accomplish a goal. For each step the user takes, a use case documents the system's response to the user's action. By documenting a user's interaction and the associated system response, use cases can be a very effective way to document system requirements that take into consideration a user's needs and interactions when accomplishing a task.

Researching Your Users

In the midst of defining, understanding and documenting user characteristics, the question usually arises, "What if I don't know who my user audience is?" or "What if I know who my audience is, but I don't know very much about them?"

User Type: Operator of a Fingerprint Device

When this occurs, there are several ways to go about learning about your users:

1. Begin by interviewing key stakeholders within the organization. Ask leadership and managers who they believe the target user audiences are.

2. Review existing data about your user population, including past results from surveys, focus groups, interviews, etc.
3. Conduct new research to learn about your audience.

Table 3. User Tasks and Prioritization

Task	Frequency of Use?	Importance to User?	Importance to Business Objectives?	Feasibility?	Vulnerability to Usability Issues?
1. Collect demographic data from each user, including: gender, date of birth, and country of origin.	*High*	*High*	*To be completed in the User and Business Requirements Phase*	*To be completed in the Design Phase*	*To be completed in the Evaluation Phase*
2. Collect biometric sample (fingerprint).	*High*	*High*			
3. Assist users with questions about the system.	*High*	*High*			
4. Trouble-shoot system errors.	*High*	*High*			
5. Register each individual user and establish user identity within the database.	*High*	*High*			

Conducting research with users is an essential step in the user-centered design process. There are numerous ways to learn about your users at this stage of the process, including[2]:

- User Surveys
- Focus Groups
- User Interviews

- Contextual Inquiry / Naturalistic Observation
- Cognitive Walkthroughs
- Usability Testing

While primary research directly with users is far superior to the opinions of colleagues and management, it is not always feasible to conduct this type of research. Sometimes access to users of biometric systems can be limited or resources/time do not allow for primary research to be performed. In these instances, it is best to talk with stakeholders within your organization who have had direct contact with users and to learn all that you can through this second-hand interaction.

Remember, time spent in the early planning phases learning about users generally saves time and development costs in the later phases, when usability issues are much more costly and time-consuming to fix.

CONCLUSION

A thorough analysis of your existing biometric system and users' interaction or context of use with that system is a critical first step to designing a truly usable system. By understanding your users and their tasks with a system, including how their demographics, abilities and environment affect the use of a biometric system, and its eventual success, your project team will be better positioned to develop a successful product.

This in-depth understanding of a biometric system's context of use is key to identifying the user and organizational requirements that will ultimately impact the design and development. The following chapter will discuss how to use the information analyzed in the Context of Use phase to develop user requirements that will ultimately impact the performance of the system and the resulting success of the organization.

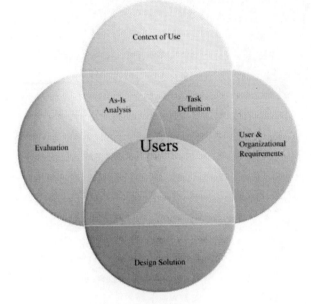

Figure 7. Components of the Context of Use Phase

5. USER & ORGANIZATIONAL REQUIREMENTS

Determine Requirements

The requirements phase of the development lifecycle typically occurs after the product team has established a thorough understanding of the biometric system's context of use and users.

The goal of any requirements analysis phase is to create clear, unambiguous requirements for a biometric system so that the entire development team thoroughly understands what the system should do and how it should work. There are many types of requirements including:

- Business and Organizational Requirements
- Environmental and Physical Requirements
- Functional Requirements
- Nonfunctional Requirements
- Technical and System Requirements
- User Requirements

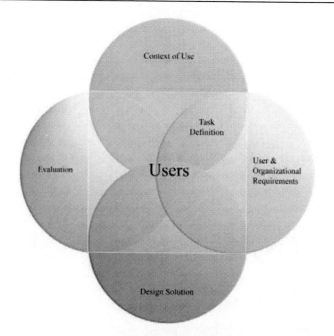
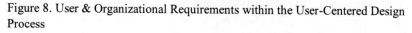

Figure 8. User & Organizational Requirements within the User-Centered Design Process

Each of these types of requirements may have usability components, in addition to other requirements. The requirements suggested in this document are not meant to be all-encompassing, but simply highlight some of the potential usability issues that may be documented.

Understanding Different Types of Requirement

Requirements analysis can be quite detailed with varying levels of complexity.

Many teams may find themselves with several types of requirements documents, while other teams may only have one requirements document.

No matter the number of requirements documents, it's important that your requirements address the key factors affecting your design. In the following section, we will discuss some of the types of requirements you may want to consider for your biometric project.

User Requirements are requirements that are based on the needs of the users.

Business and Organizational Requirements are requirements that the organization has for a product or system. These requirements are typically established to help the organization achieve its business goals and are usually focused on high-level business objectives.

Environmental and Physical Requirements are requirements about the physical environment that the system will be used in, or the context of use. These requirements are established to ensure that design teams take into consideration the physical attributes of the environment, including location, lighting, noise levels, etc.

Functional Requirements are requirements that specify the features and functions that the system will support. In short, the functional specifications identify the tasks necessary to fulfill the business requirements. While, the high-level business requirements specify the "why," the detailed functional specifications identify the "what." It is important to note that functional requirements do *not* specify the "how." Determining how to fulfill a requirement is something that is determined during the design phase.

Nonfunctional Requirements are requirements that cannot be described by a single feature or function. They are broader requirements for the product/system and may include things such as look and feel requirements, usability requirements, performance requirements, social requirements, legal requirements, etc. Although nonfunctional requirements are not tied to a specific feature or function and are used to describe the overall attributes and characteristics of a system, they can lead to more specific functional requirements.

Technical and System Requirements are requirements that detail the technical environment that the system will be built on, including hardware and software requirements. These requirements may also include items such as security needs, database structures, supported platforms, etc.

The following sections will describe each of these types of requirements in greater detail.

User Requirements

First and foremost, it is essential to document user requirements. These requirements should document what the system is required to do to meet users' needs, not what the system requires of a user. It is important to note that users should not be required to have specific skills to use a system. As designers of biometric systems, it is essential that we understand our users' characteristics and any implications for biometric system requirements.

At this point in the process, re-visit the user analysis you completed for each audience and review the potential user requirements identified. Ensure that all of the requirements documents created address users' needs and requirements.

BUSINESS AND ORGANIZATIONAL REQUIREMENTS

In any technology environment, it is essential to ensure that the product developed meets the needs of the organization, as well as the needs of the users. The business requirements help to specify what the organization wants to achieve. Many times, business requirements are fairly high-level and do not address specific functionality.

Example business requirements:

- To create a system that will accurately and efficiently collect biometric samples.
- To reduce the number of system errors.
- To design an intuitive interface that will decrease the amount of assistance/help required to use the biometric device.

In order to determine the organizational requirements, begin by posing the following questions to your management team:

- What is the purpose of the system?
- What are the goals for the product?
- How would you describe the system?
  - From an organization's standpoint?
  - From a user's standpoint?
- What outcomes would you like to achieve?

- How would you define a successful system for your organization?

Once you've created a list of goals for your biometric system or product, try to see how well your organization's goals match up with the goals you identified for your users. It's is critical to the success of the product that the goals are closely aligned.

For instance:

Organization's Purpose / Goals	Users' Purpose / Goals
• To create a system that will collect accurate biometric samples in the most efficient manner possible, with the highest possible throughput.	• To quickly pass through customs and border patrols with as little inconvenience as possible.

In the example above, it's easy to see that the organization has a desire to process individuals as efficiently as possible, just as users have a desire to complete the task as quickly as they can. In this instance, both parties want an efficient system that will speed users through the process.

Mapping organizational goals to user goals is a key step in the process to ensure that the system you are designing will meet both the needs of your organization and the needs of your users.

Functional Requirements

Functional requirements define what a biometric system must do; they do not specify how the system will be implemented.

In defining these requirements, it is essential to re-visit the user tasks identified in earlier stages of the user-centered design process. By considering users' tasks and their context of use, it is easier for design teams to develop workflows and requirements that will meet the needs of users and ultimately help improve the usability of a biometric system. In defining functional requirements, begin by clearly stating the goal of the system. An example:

The system shall provide feedback to a user to let him/her know when an acceptable sample is captured.

Note that the requirement states the goal of the system, but does not define how the biometric system will provide feedback. This decision is left to the design team to make once they have had an opportunity to review all of the system requirements.

Once all of the functional requirements are written down, you will want to formally document these requirements. There are several ways to document your functional requirements, including: use cases, Unified Modeling Language (UML), process diagrams, task flow diagrams, task scenarios, etc. Since many of the requirements documents are quite detailed, it is essential to document each feature step-by-step. By breaking down each task into its subparts and creating task workflows, it is easier to create a functional specification that more closely matches the needs and experiences of users.

Nonfunctional Requirements

Nonfunctional requirements identify requirements for a system that are not specifically tied to a feature or function. They may include:

- Graphic design requirements (or look and feel) – *The design of the system must reflect the corporate branding of the organization.*

- Usability requirements – *At least 75% of users will be able to successfully use the system without assistance or help.*

- User Experience – *The system will provide users with a consistent interface, interactions and affordances.*

- Performance requirements – *The system will accurately collect samples from 90% of users on the first attempt.*

- Social requirements –*The system shall mitigate users' perceived health risks of biometric devices.*

- Legal requirements – *The system shall protect the privacy of the end users who submit samples.*

Nonfunctional requirements help to guide the development of the overall system.

Environmental and Physical Requirements

Based on a review of the context of use, environmental requirements should be created to address the attributes and characteristics of the physical location where the system will be located.

These requirements may involve determining the optimal height of a biometric device, defining interaction styles based on noise and lighting levels, and/or specifying space and furniture requirements.

While these requirements primarily depend on an evaluation of the physical surroundings, it is also important to review how users are affected by environmental factors and adjust the physical design of a biometric system based on users' characteristics. For instance, the optimal height of a biometric device should be based upon a thorough evaluation of the physical environment where the device will be located, but also should take into consideration common anthropometrics, such as the average the height of your user population. Additionally, these decisions should also be supplemented by observation of users in real-world settings to evaluate users' posture, as well as how users of differing heights utilize the system. Based on an analysis of these factors, a suitable height should be defined and included in the requirements documentation.

Additionally, it may be necessary to develop a distinct set of environmental requirements for *each* physical location in which a product/system will be located. For instance, a noisy environment may require different requirements than a quiet location, just as a system located under low light may have different requirements than a system which is in direct sunlight.

Below are some example requirements for different types of environmental factors:

- *Noisy Environment*
  A requirement could be that the system relies on visual and other types of non- auditory feedback, as users may not be able to hear audio feedback in a noisy location.

- *Low Light*
  A requirement may specify that interaction screens, visual cues and colored displays are bright enough to be seen in locations with poor lighting. Or the requirement could require that supplemental lighting be provided to adequately light the system.

- *Natural Light*
  A requirement may stipulate that in outdoor settings, it is best to rely on audio and other types of sensory feedback as the direct sunlight might produce a glare, making it difficult to see visual feedback. Or the requirement could entail developing screens that do not reflect light and reduce the amount of glare. Another requirement could be to use screen filters as a way to reduce the potential problems of glare.

- *Temperature and Humidity*
  A requirement might state that the system is able to sustain extreme temperatures and high levels of humidity. Or the requirement may state that the system must operate within a range of temperatures and humidity.

In each of the above examples, there may be more than one way to address an issue and therefore, the implementation may vary from project to project.

Additionally, since devices may be used under a variety of conditions and in a plethora of locations, it is essential to review the physical attributes of each location and define common environmental requirements to address the differing needs.

Technical and System Requirements

In developing your biometric system, it is also essential to document the hardware and software systems upon which the product will be based. The requirements should identify any issues or constraints regarding the technical environment and should also specify system requirements for the security and maintenance of the device.

Researching Your Requirements

In order to understand and document the requirements for your biometric system, you will need to have a thorough understanding of:

- Your user audience
- Your organization and management objectives

- Your current system and goals for future improvements
- Your competitors' products

Additionally, you should be aware of the environmental, physical, social, and technical factors affecting your system. Armed with this knowledge, you should be able to create clear, unambiguous requirements which will drive the design and development of a usable biometric device.

In order to ensure you have adequate information to write and develop effective requirements, consider conducting the following types of research: [3]

- User Surveys
- Focus Groups
- User Interviews (including interviews with internal leadership)
- Contextual Interviews/Naturalistic Observation
- Cognitive Walkthroughs
- Expert Reviews
- Competitive Analysis
- Usability Testing

CONCLUSION

In order to identify and define the requirements of your system, it is essential that biometric project teams take into consideration many types of requirements, including:

- user requirements,
- business and organizational requirements,
- environmental and physical requirements,
- functional requirements,
- nonfunctional requirements, and
- technical and system requirements.

To define these requirements, it is critical that you have a clear understanding of your users, their context of use and the tasks that they will use the system for. The design decisions that you make based upon the requirements set forth will ultimately have a great impact on the user experience of the system.

The following chapter will provide additional detail on designing a usable system that not only improves the user experience, but also improves system performance and throughput.

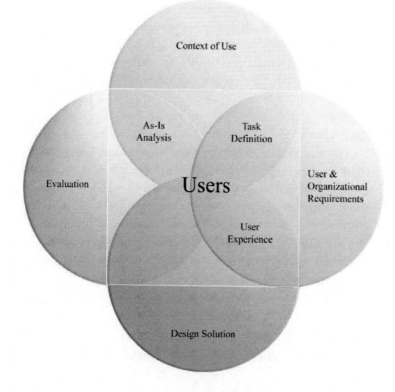

Figure 9. Components of the User & Organizational Requirements Phase

6. DESIGN SOLUTION

Develop the Design

Once the requirements have been identified, the design team can begin to evaluate ways to address each requirement and specify a design solution. The design solution should encompass the entire product/system including the design that end users will interact with, as well as the design that operators and

system analysts will use. It is important to note that the design considerations should not be limited to end users, but should also take into consideration those users who will be operating the systems and analyzing the data.

When considering solutions for the system design (hardware/software), the interface design (the way the system will interact with users); instructional design (method and materials presented prior to users approaching the system); and training/support design (help materials for end users and operators to effectively use the system), consider the following two questions:

- What are the needs of my end users (or the individuals providing a sample)?
- What are the needs of the operators /analysts managing the system?

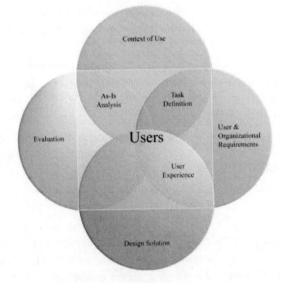

Figure 10. Design Solution within the User-Centered Design Process

Collectively, these design elements help to comprise the system's use experience..

When considering the design of a solution, it is important to consider both the interaction design, as well as the interface design. Ideally, these design elements work together to provide a seamless experience for users (both end users and system users).

Interaction Design

Simply put, interaction design is a method used to define the way a system responds to a user's actions. The goal of interaction design is to define the behavior of a system, without implying any look and feel (or interface design) requirements. The interaction design is the foundation upon which the interface design will be built.

This process involves several steps that focus on the tasks a system will perform. To begin:

- Define the tasks that the system will perform, based on the task analysis conducted during the Context of Use and User and Organizational Requirements phases.
- Review each task and identify the sub-steps of each task.
- Identify user interactions for each task and the associated system response.
- Create a use case or workflow diagram to document these tasks and interactions.
- Define how the system will work for each step in your task flow or workflow diagram.

To simplify the process, begin with a very simple task and work your way to more difficult or complex tasks a system will perform. For each task, ask yourself:

- When will this process begin?
- What initiates the process? Does a user initiate a process, if so, how?
- How does the system respond to a user's action? What type of information does the system need to communicate with a user so that the user knows what to do next?
- When does the process end? How will the user know that the task is finished and that it was successful?
- If the task is not successful, how will the user know that there was an error? What types of feedback or messages will the system communicate to a user to help them correct the error and complete the task successfully?

These questions all focus on ensuring that the user and the system are working together, in a partnership, with the same end goal. Each step of the

process is considered from a user's viewpoint as well as from a system viewpoint, taking care to identify the types of feedback needed to keep the interaction moving along.

Interaction design is similar to a conversation; a conversation between the user and the system. For each action a user makes, the system must respond. Thus, a solid interaction design specification is needed. This process takes into consideration how a system should behave throughout an entire task and also tries to consider the possibility for errors along the way.

At each point in the process, an error can occur. A user may become confused and not know what to do next, a user may not be able to tell when a task is finished, or a user may prematurely think a task is completed before it actually is. Numerous types of errors may occur at any point in the process. Therefore, it is necessary to consider how a system will work to avoid errors, and when errors do happen, how the system will provide feedback to a user, so that the user may continue the task. It is this type of feedback or conversation that is necessary for the system and the user to work in partnership toward the end goal.

For instance, let's look at the task of a user providing a sample. First consider:

- When does the task begin? Does it begin when a user places his/her finger on a fingerprint reader? Or does it begin much earlier when a user, waiting in line, reads posters or other instructional guides before approaching a system?
- What types of messages does the system provide the user so that the user knows what to do? How does the system communicate to the user so that the user knows how to provide a sample?
- Once the user initiates the task, what types of feedback does the system provide to the user to let him know that he is positioning his hand/finger appropriately?
- How does the system let the user know when the sample has been successfully captured?
- If there is an error, what types of feedback are provided? Does the system let the user know that the quality is poor? Or that the positioning was off? Or that a user needs to apply more/less pressure? What types of tips or guidance are provided so that a user can correct the error?

These are the types of questions that biometric system designers need to consider when defining an interaction specification.

To create a successful interaction design for a biometric system, developers need to think of each task as a conversation between the user and the system. Each step within the process needs to be considered so that a user and a system can successfully exchange information to accomplish a task. This information should be documented in an interaction design specification which will serve as the foundation for the interface design.

Interface Design

During the interaction design stage, the team focuses on "what" the system will communicate and "when" it will communicate with users, whereas, the interface design stage defines "how" the system will communicate with the user.

At this point in the process, biometric developers begin to think about the best way to communicate with users. Designers may consider many design options, such as:

- Should the system provide a graphical interface or menu structure to users?
- Should textual messages be provided on the screen?
- Should the biometric device provide visual cues, such as lights or other cues?
- Should it provide audible cues?
- Should the hardware be shaped in a specific way (i.e. conformed to the shape of a finger to signal how a user should position her hand)?

All of these design questions are focused on the interface and how the interface will work. When considering the interface design, it is important to consider providing feedback to users in multiple ways. If a system relies on only one method to provide feedback, it may fail to meet the needs of users who cannot understand the method selected. For instance:

- If a system uses text to communicate to users, which language should be used? Will the system support multiple languages? Will Braille be provided?

- If a system provides visual cues, will those cues be visible during daylight hours if a system is used outdoors (i.e. border crossings)? How will blind or visually impaired users interact with this type of system?
- If the system uses lights or colors to signal success, are the colors chosen universally understood? For instance, if red is chosen to signal an error, does this color communicate across nationalities and cultures?
- If a system relies on audible cues, will those cues be heard in noisy environments such as airport security lines? How will hearing-impaired users interact with the system?
- If a system is shaped or contoured to help users position their hands/fingers, will that shape accommodate different hand shapes and sizes? Will it be positioned so that tall individuals as well as shorter individuals can reach it? How will individuals in wheelchairs be accommodated?

The design of a user interface is a complex process that must consider not only the content of a message, but also the most effective way to deliver that message.

CONCLUSION

Since there are so many ways to design a system, it is helpful to try out several different designs and evaluate the success of each design with users. That way, the best elements from each design can be merged into the end-resulting biometric system.

By involving users early on in this process when it is still easy to make changes to a design, biometric system designs can have a much more measurable impact on a system's usability. Waiting until the end to solicit user feedback is dangerous, as many times the feedback is received too late to make any substantial changes.

Additionally, we've found that users are also much more willing to give critical feedback about a rough prototype that is still in design and are less likely to be critical about a fully functioning system. This is yet another reason to solicit feedback during the early stages of the design process.

The design process should, in fact, be seen as an iterative process, whereby prototypes are evaluated with users and revised until a system is measurably easier to use.

This process ensures that the system is being developed with users in mind and helps to prevent any show-stopping issues from being discovered too late in the process.

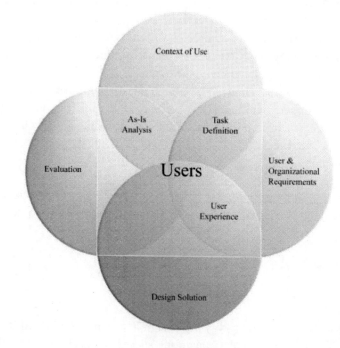

Figure 11. Components of the Design Solution Phase

7. EVALUATION

Conduct the Evaluation

Evaluation is an essential part of any project development lifecycle. It ensures that the design is on the right track and helps to identify issues that still need to be resolved.

A well-conducted and well-planned project will have several rounds of evaluation, at varying levels of fidelity. By incorporating user feedback throughout the design of a system, it is easier to identify major problems or flaws in a system at a much earlier stage. In the diagram below, it is important to note that the evaluation and design stages overlap.

Too often, design teams consider evaluation to be the final stage and wait to conduct any type of system evaluation until the entire system is nearing completion. This presents several risks. One major risk is that the evaluation may reveal major issues with the system that are too costly or too difficult to make in the latter stages of development. Therefore, we strongly suggest an iterative design process, wherein biometric project teams share design concepts with users in the early stages of development, when it is easier to make design changes.

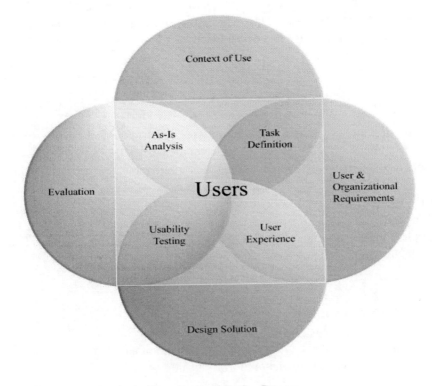

Figure 12. Evaluation in the User-Centered Design Process

ITERATIVE DESIGN & EVALUATION

In an iterativee design process, users are asked to review concepts throughout the design process and based on the results of the evaluation, the design is revised in order to improve user performance and satisfaction.

In order to involve users as early as possible, users may be asked to evaluate low-fidelity designs or even a series of paper prototypes. As the design process evolves, the fidelity of the prototypes is also likely to progress and eventually result in a high fidelity test of a functioning system.

It is also important to note, that the number of users involved in these evaluation processes it typically much lower than that required to test for performance measurements. Whereas it may require hundreds of thousands of users to test a system's performance for captures, a usability evaluation may include as few as eight users. The small sample size required to conduct usability evaluations makes it much more realistic to conduct several iterative tests throughout the design and development of a biometric system or device.

TYPES OF EVALUATION

During the design and evaluation phases, the types and frequency of the evaluation may vary. At the earlier stages of the design, the evaluation may be more qualitative, where users are asked their impressions or reactions to initial designs. In the latter stages of development, biometric systems may be tested with users in a more quantitative usability test, where users' performance using the system is measured.

It is important to note that the best approach to evaluation combines both qualitative and quantitative evaluations.

Qualitative Feedback

Qualitative feedback is important in the design of any system. This type of feedback may come in a variety of forms, including:

- Asking users about their expectations of what the system will do and how it will function

- Observing users interacting with a system while 'thinking aloud' and noting areas that cause user confusion or frustration
- Probing for suggestions from users and asking users about their level of satisfaction with the system

Users' comments and concerns can be an extremely important way to learn whether or not the design of the system matches users' expectations of how the system should act. Although users' comments can be extremely informative, it is also essential to understand how well users can perform using the system in order to quantitatively measure the effectiveness of a design.

Quantitative Feedback

In order to evaluate the success of a design it is important to measure how well users are able to accomplish tasks using the system. Examples of quantitative measures that may be measured include:

- **Task Completion Rates:** Percent of users who successfully complete each task

- **Time on Task:** Time it takes for users to perform a task from beginning to end

- **Error Rates:** Number of errors made during the course of a task

- **Satisfaction Rating:** Satisfaction scores for the system

Many biometric design teams will begin the design process with a quantitative usability test, known as a baseline or benchmark usability test. The results of this test are used to measure the effectiveness of future design improvements. Many teams use the Common Industry Format (CIF) (ISO/IEC 25062:2006) to document the performance of the system. The CIF provides a standard way for organizations to present and report quantitative data gathered in a formal test. This report can be used as a benchmark for future comparisons.

Following the benchmark test, design teams typically revise the system to improve the system's effectiveness and efficiency. Once the changes have been made, the design team may repeat the same test methodology as the

baseline test in order to determine if the changes have made a measureable impact. Typically, design teams hope that the changes improved users' success rates, decreased the time it takes to perform a task, decreased the number of errors made by users, and increased users' satisfaction with the system.

It is these types of metrics that can help a design team stay focused on making data-driven, performance-based improvements. In this environment, project teams try to make recommendations for improvement that they believe will improve the performance of the system and have a measureable impact on the effectiveness and efficiency of the system's design.

To learn more about usability testing, please see the chapter on usability methods.

CONCLUSION

Evaluation is a critical component of any design process and product improvement lifecycle. Without continual feedback from users, design teams suffer and end up operating blindly, not knowing whether design recommendations will actually improve the usability or a biometric system or worse case, make the system more difficult/confusing to use.

Armed with the results of an evaluation, design teams can operate much more efficiently and can focus their energy on design changes that will have the greatest impact on user performance and satisfaction, placing less emphasis on cosmetic changes that may only have a minor impact on the performance of their system. Teams that are able to effectively and accurately prioritize resources are much more cost-effective and productive in the long run.

8. USABILITY METHODS

The following sections will provide information on various usability techniques and research methods including:

- As-Is Analysis
- Cognitive Walkthroughs
- Competitive Analysis
- Contextual Inquiries / Naturalistic Observation

- Expert Reviews
- Focus Groups
- Parallel Design
- Usability Testing
- User Interviews
- User Surveys

As-Is Analysis

What Is This method?

An As-Is Analysis is a complete evaluation of the existing system in its current state.

When Should It Be Used?

It is important to conduct an As-Is Analysis at the beginning of any project in order to better understand the current system, its strengths and its weaknesses. By conducting a thorough analysis of the existing system, design teams can effectively develop system requirements and design solutions that better meet the needs of users. These 'targeted' design decisions will be much more effective in designing a usable, user-friendly product.

While it is critical to conduct an As-Is Analysis at the beginning of any large design project, it is also essential to continually evaluate the design of your system throughout the entire project lifecycle. By continually monitoring the quality of your product, you are in a much better position to implement improvements that will have a measurable impact.

How Do You Conduct an As-Is Analysis?

An As-Is Analysis should collectively evaluate and measure as many facets of a product as possible. This may mean that you need to gather data from multiple sources, including:

Performance   Throughput

data	Ratio of submissions to successful captures
Observational data	How do users currently use the system? When do they struggle? Which aspects of the system cause confusion or frustration?
User Feedback	Do users request assistance? What is the most common concern or frequently asked question? Do users use the help documents or instructional guides provided? If so, how? Do users require training? If so, where do they struggle the most?
User Interviews and Surveys	What do users think of the system? Which aspects do they believe are the most difficult to use? What suggestions for improvement can your users offer?
Usability Testing	Which aspects of the system are the most difficult to use? Which are the easiest to use? What causes users to struggle? What improvements can be made to address these issues?
Expert Reviews	Which areas of the system do usability experts believe are vulnerable to usability issues?
Competitive Analysis	How does your product compare to your competitors? Are there aspects of your competitors' products that perform better than yours? How can you create a product that will outperform that of your competition?

What Are the Benefits/Limitations?

An As-Is Analysis takes into consideration all of the types of feedback and evaluation conducted on your system to give design teams an overarching view of the system. This process is an extremely useful process and one that can be used to benchmark the performance of your existing system, so that the success of future design changes can be measured and quantified.

With a broad knowledge of the various facets of your system and your users, development teams can effectively target design decisions and changes. When requirements and design decisions are not based upon this deep foundation of knowledge, design teams are operating blindly, making choices that may or may not impact the actual system performance. Many teams have labored over system requirements and the various ways to implement a particular feature or function, only to have expended a lot of time, energy and resources on a feature that will not truly have an impact on the ultimate performance of a system and the users of that system.

It is critical to conduct a thorough As-Is Analysis, in order to make targeted, effective design decisions that will enhance the ease of use, reduce system complexity, improve user performance and satisfaction, and reduce support and training costs.

COGNITIVE WALKTHROUGHS

What Is This Method?

Cognitive walkthroughs are an 'inspection' method (which means that actual users are not involved in the process). It is a method in which a usability expert or a group of experts inspect the system by walking through a set of tasks as a user would, noting any problems or difficulties a user may encounter. Although typically conducted by a usability expert, cognitive walkthroughs can be conducted by anyone with a thorough understanding of the system including software engineers, system designers/developers, documentation specialists, subject matter experts, etc.

When Should It Be Used?

Cognitive walkthroughs can be performed at any stage of design but typically occur during the early design stages and may be conducted on paper prototypes, low-fidelity prototypes or fully functioning biometric systems.

How Do You Conduct a Cognitive Walkthrough?

The first step to conducting a Cognitive Walkthrough is to review the data gathered and analyzed during the Context of Use and User/Organizational Requirements phases. To conduct a Cognitive Walkthrough, begin by answering the following questions:

Users   Who are the users of your biometric system?
                     Who are the primary users? Secondary users?
                     Consider all aspects of use, including the end user, the system operator and the system analyst.

                     Now select one user type for your cognitive review.
Tasks   What tasks will users perform using the system?
                     Is this a repeat task for users?
                     What type of knowledge will users have going into this task? What is their experience with the system?
                     Once you have selected a set of tasks to evaluate, you must break each task down into its sub-parts. By breaking the task down into smaller sequential steps, it is easier to tell when the system does not meet users' expectations.

Once you have selected a user profile and a task, the individuals conducting the Cognitive Walkthrough use the system to perform the task as though they were seeing the system through the eyes of the user. By stepping into the role of the user, the experts evaluate the system looking for issues or problems that users may encounter.

What Are the Benefits/Limitations?

Cognitive Walkthroughs can be very good at helping to identify potential usability issues early in the design phases. In order for the walkthroughs to be effective, it is essential that the individual or team conducting the walkthrough has a thorough understanding of the users in order to simulate their experiences with the system.

It should be noted that since Cognitive Walkthroughs are an inspection technique and do not involve real-world users, experts may not always pick up on subtleties in a design that could impact a user. While this technique does help to focus the design on the needs of users, it should not be the only user-centered methodology employed, as expert evaluations cannot replace the value of real-world input from users.

COMPETITIVE ANALYSIS

What Is This Method?

A Competitive Analysis is a technique that is used to evaluate the systems of your competition so that you may learn from others' design decisions and understand how another organization is attempting to fill a similar need. In the simplest of terms, you compare and contrast your system with that of your competition.

When Should It Be Used?

Competitive Analysis can be conducted at any stage of the product lifecycle. It is typically important to conduct a Competitive Analysis if you are planning to make some improvements to your system or when your competitors release updates to their systems.

How Do You Conduct a Competitive Analysis?

There are several ways to perform a Competitive Analysis, ranging from very informal to very formal. In conducting a Competitive Analysis, begin by

identifying your 'competition.' It's important to think outside of the box for this part of the process, as there may be others who are providing similar, but not identical services. By looking for examples from others, it is wise to gather a broad sample from several different products and systems.

A Competitive Analysis can be as formal or as informal as you would like it to be. It can be as informal as simply reviewing competitors' systems to identify the differences between the products. Or, it can be more formal, in that you actually conduct a Cognitive Walkthrough, contextual inquiry, expert review, focus group, usability test, user interview or user survey on the competing system. Depending on the detail needed, it is possible to conduct a blind A/B comparison, wherein users are asked about two (or more) products and asked to compare the systems. In this type of evaluation, it is essential that users do not know the affiliation of the person or group of people conducting the evaluation, as this knowledge may bias users' comments and performance. This type of A/B comparison can be extremely helpful in identifying which design options elicit improved user performance and decreased user frustration.

What Are the Benefits/Limitations?

This technique is an extremely valuable way to learn about various design solutions before investing time and resources on system improvements. Not only does this method help project teams to improve upon good designs and to avoid design solutions that are not effective, it also helps teams to build a better understanding of the existing marketplace and the types of products and systems that users will be interacting with.

Since users will inevitably learn from their interactions with other systems and will make assumptions about the way your system should work based upon these previous experiences, it is important to have a thorough understanding of your competitors' products.

Armed with this information, project teams will have the necessary resources to make informed design decisions.

CONTEXTUAL INQUIRY/NATURALISTIC OBSERVATION

What Is This Method?

Contextual Inquiry is a method that allows you to observe users in a real-world environment, performing tasks as they would if they were not being observed. In contrast to other techniques such as usability testing, user interviews, user surveys, and focus groups, the evaluator travels to the user to observe them in a naturalistic setting and allows the user to 'drive' the session.

Contextual Inquiries take into consideration the entire process including the initial approach, instructional guides, physical and environmental conditions, situational factors, hardware design, software design, etc. It evaluates the entire process in order to provide a complete view of how users interact with a system in a real-world context.

When Should It Be Used?

Contextual Inquiries can be conducted at any stage of the process, but typically tend to be performed on a fully functioning system.

How Do You Conduct a Contextual Inquiry?

During a Contextual Inquiry, a usability expert or team of experts typically travel to observe users in a real-world environment, such as an airport or border crossing. Although typically conducted by a usability professional, the inquiry can be conducted by anyone with a thorough knowledge of the system and the system's users.

The individual performing the inquiry is typically very passive, allowing users to act naturally as though they were not being observed. During the inquiry, the usability expert may ask questions to better understand a user's actions, but typically questions are held until the end to avoid interrupting a user's normal workflow. The person performing the inquiry may also ask for permission to tape the sessions so that they may capture the entire process and conduct an in-depth review following the inquiry.

This process should be repeated with several users under varying conditions in order to identify trends in users, in the environment, and with the technology.

Following the observations, the individual conducting the evaluation will summarize their observations, noting workarounds or shortcuts that users have created, itemizing instances where users deviated from the expected workflow, listing features that performed well, as well as features that were difficult for users to understand.

What Are the Benefits/Limitations?

The benefit of a Contextual Inquiry is that you have an opportunity to observe users in the environment in which they will use the system. It helps to identify design issues that may arise because of environmental factors (i.e. the noise level in an airport may be too loud for users to hear audible cues that tested just fine in a usability lab) physical conditions (i.e. instructional guides that are positioned too far in advance of a system that users forget what to do by the time they reach the device) or occurrences (unexpected interruptions of the biometric process).

It is this type of subtle, but extremely important information that Contextual Inquires help to uncover.

One of the drawbacks to this technique is that there is sometimes so much data to analyze that it becomes a very time-consuming and labor-intensive effort.

EXPERT REVIEW

What Is This Method?

An Expert Review is similar to a Cognitive Walkthrough in that it is conducted by an expert or team of experts. The main difference between a Cognitive Walkthrough and an Expert Review is that an Expert Review evaluates a system against a set of best practices, design guidelines, and standards.

Expert Reviews are sometimes referred to as Heuristic Reviews as evaluators may choose to evaluate a system according to a set of heuristics (or design principles) such as Jakob Nielsen's 10 heuristic guidelines. (Nielsen)

When Should It Be Used?

Expert Reviews can be conducted at any stage of the process and may be conducted on a paper prototype, low-fidelity prototype or fully functioning system.

How Do You Conduct an Expert Review?

During an Expert Review, a usability professional or team of usability professionals reviews the system for adherence to design guidelines and heuristics, noting where the system fails to meet certain standards. Based on the review, the usability professional will provide a set of recommendations and suggestions for improvement.

What Are the Benefits/Limitations?

An Expert Review is a method that can be performed fairly quickly and inexpensively. However, just like the Cognitive Review, it is important to note that the review is being done by an expert or team of experts. Since experts do not have the same experiences and perspectives as users, they sometimes miss usability issues or identify issues that are 'false alarms' (issues that are not really usability issues).

In an effort to offset potential misses and false alarms, it is generally recommended that more than one individual be involved in an Expert Review. One approach is to have a team of usability experts conduct the review independently of each other and then share the issues they identified. The list of issues can then be reviewed to find issues that were identified by multiple usability professionals. While not a perfect solution, this principle can help to ensure that the most commonly identified issues are fixed first.

Like all 'inspection' methods, it is recommended that project teams also involve users in the design and development of any biometric system.

FOCUS GROUP

What Is This Method?

A Focus Group is a large group interview or discussion that allows project teams to explore opinions and gather feedback from users.

When Should It Be Used?

Focus Groups tend to be very useful at the beginning of a design project to gather information about users' needs and to ask for feedback on initial design concepts. However, Focus Groups do not tend to be a good evaluation technique, in that it is very difficult to gather meaningful data from a group evaluation. Since users will be using a system as individuals, it is much more helpful to gather this type of information in one-on-one interviews or usability testing.

How Do You Conduct a Focus Group?

To conduct a Focus Group, first begin by recruiting a group of users (8 – 12) who represent your user population. Next, select a moderator or facilitator. The moderator should be someone who can objectively ask questions of the group and is not tied to one particular design concept. It is also critical that the moderator be a skilled leader in order to drive the conversation of the group and ensure that each focus group participant has an opportunity to voice his/her opinions.

During the Focus Group, the moderator may ask users about previous experiences with biometric devices, may try to probe into any issues or concerns users have had in the past, and finally may try to present some design ideas/concepts to gather the group's feedback.

The Focus Groups may be recorded or observed by other team members through a one-way mirror. Following the Focus Groups, the team will summarize the findings and recommendations resulting from the sessions.

What Are the Benefits/Limitations?

Focus Groups are a good way to quickly gather data from several users within a user segment. They can be a helpful way to gauge users' opinions and gather early feedback on design concepts, however, they tend not to be as useful in the latter stages of the design, when other techniques such as usability testing are more effective.

PARALLEL DESIGN

What Is This Method?

Parallel Design is a method that enables large teams to generate many design concepts quickly in an attempt to bring the best design concepts forward by saturating the design space.

In short, it is a method that asks designers to each independently create a design. The group then shares their ideas and designers are asked to iterate their design concepts by improving upon the ideas shared. This technique helps designers to quickly build off concepts presented by their colleagues, and with each iteration, improve upon the ideas presented.

When Should It Be Used?

Parallel Design should be used at the beginning of any design phase that will result in major changes to a system. It is a technique that works best in the early stages of a project.

How Do You Conduct a Parallel Design Session?

Parallel Design sessions are a great way to generate a lot of design ideas very quickly. During a Parallel Design session, various members of the project team identify a particular feature that needs improvement and then focus their attention on creating a useful, usable solution. The session should include various members from the project team and can be conducted with graphic designers, hardware/software engineers, usability professionals, marketing

specialists, documentation writers, etc. The sessions can be conducted with as few as three participants and with as many as a team feels comfortable including. A group of around 10- 20 members tends to be just about right.

During the design session, the team will begin by discussing the feature to be designed (or redesigned). It is essential that the team discuss the users of the system, as well as the tasks to be completed. Lastly, the team should review any data gathered from other usability methods, including user interviews, usability tests, competitive analysis, expert reviews, etc.

Once the team has agreed upon the users and tasks, as well as some of the key requirements for the feature, each member of the group is asked to independently create a design. Once the designs are created, they are shared with the group. One easy way to share the designs is to have each person create their design on a large piece of paper and then post the paper prototypes around the perimeter of the room so that everyone can walk around the room and review the concepts.

After everyone has had a chance to review the concepts, the individual members are again asked to independently create a new design. In the new design, the parallel design participants are asked to integrate the best concepts from the other designs and attempt to improve each concept. After the designs are completed, they are once again posted for the group to review. This process can be repeated several times throughout a one or two-day session.

At the conclusion of the session, the group should select the best concepts from the designs presented and build one to two optimal design solutions.

What Are the Benefits/Limitations?

Not only is this technique an effective way to quickly generate as many design ideas as possible, but it is also a very effective way to continually improve on the ideas of others in collaborative and cooperative fashion. By including team members from various parts of your project team, design ideas that are not normally thought of by a single system designer can have a very positive impact on the overall design of a system.

Additionally, this technique is a very useful way to gather buy-in from stakeholders throughout your organization, as team members feel as though they have had a part in creating the design of the system.

USABILITY TESTING

What Is This Method?

Usability Testing is an evaluation method that asks real-world users to 'try out' or test a design of a system, while a usability professional notes areas where users struggle or make mistakes. Sessions may be recorded or observed by members of the design team in order to identify usability issues with the system.

When Should It Be Used?

Usability Testing is a technique that should be used throughout the entire design lifecycle. It can be conducted on paper prototypes, low-fidelity prototypes and fully functioning systems.

How Do You Conduct a Usability Test?

To conduct a usability test, it is important to identify the users you want to test as well as the tasks you'd like to evaluate. Once you've selected the user group you'd like to test, you'll need to recruit a representative mix of users who closely match your actual user population. Many organizations will test with eight users from each user group, while other organizations will recruit larger numbers of users. When conducting performance testing where the goal is to analyze quantitative data, you may want to recruit 30 or more users. But, if this is your first usability test, you may want to start out with eight users and then determine if you need a larger sample.

After you've defined your users, you'll want to select the tasks that you would like users to perform. Once you have a set of tasks, you'll need to translate these tasks into 'scenarios' or stories that ask a user to perform a task without actually telling a user how to do the task. The scenario should also try to avoid 'give-away' wording by not using the exact same terminology that the system does.

During the usability test, the participant works one-on-one with the facilitator. The facilitator gives the participant the scenarios one at a time and then asks the user to perform the task. During this time, the facilitator notes

areas of concern or confusion and may also ask the participant to 'think aloud' in order to better understand why a user is behaving in a certain manner.

Following the test, the design team will report the findings of the usability test. For quantitative testing, many teams use the Common Industry Format (CIF) (ISO/IEC 25062:2006) to document the performance of the system. The CIF provides a standard way for organizations to present and report quantitative data gathered in a usability test, so that it can later be compared to the results gathered in subsequent tests.

What Are the Benefits/Limitations?

Usability test sessions are an extremely valuable way to observe users interacting with your system and to note areas of concern.

Not only does usability testing provide an opportunity to observe users interacting with a system, it enables design teams to better understand why a user behaves in a certain way or why an individual is confused. By asking users to explain what they are doing as they are using the system and to probe or follow-up on interesting actions, design teams have an opportunity to see the system through the eyes of a user.

Usability testing not only provides insights into users' behavior, it also allows project teams to quantifiably measure the success of a system, including capturing metrics such as error rates, successful performance on tasks, time to complete a task, etc. This valuable data can be used to benchmark the performance of a system and subsequently measure the impact of future design improvements. In addition to the more quantitative measures, usability testing offers insights into more qualitative issues, such as the level of users' frustration, confusion, intimidation, and overall satisfaction with the system. The combination of quantitative and qualitative data can be very informative when developing recommendations to improve the system design.

While usability testing can be expensive and time-consuming it is also extremely useful in that the results are reliable and detailed.

USER INTERVIEWS

What Is This Method?

User interviews are a valuable way to learn what users think of your system in a one-on-one discussion.

When Should It Be Used?

User interviews should be conducted throughout the entire design lifecycle.

How Do You Conduct a User Interview?

User Interviews are one of the simpler user-centered design techniques. A User Interview is basically a one-on-one discussion with a user. During the interview, an interviewer may ask questions about a user's past experience with a product, a user's needs in using a specific type of biometric device, any concerns a user may have, etc. The interview may also ask users who've used the system to recall issues that they've encountered and propose ideas for improvement. Additionally, an interview may include presenting design ideas and concepts to a user and gathering feedback. This semi-structured method may explore the issues that are most important to the team at any given moment.

During an interview, the interviewer should have a basic list of questions that will be asked, but should also be able to follow-up and probe on interesting comments that a user makes. Some of the most valuable aspects of an interview can be gained from a probing question that was never part of the original interview script. Therefore, it's important that an interviewer be able to probe into interesting areas, as well as know when to bring the discussion back to the pre-defined list of questions.

What Are the Benefits/Limitations?

Interviews are a wonderful way to learn about users' opinions, feelings and reactions to a system. Users tend to be very good at telling us what isn't working on a system or identifying where they have problems, however, they tend to not be able to recommend a solution. It's important to note that users are typically not good designers, which means that interviews should be used to help better understand an issue so that a skilled team of designers can architect an effective solution. Additionally, while users may be able to explain problems that they've encountered in the past, they are typically not able to remember all of the details of the situation or the issues that it caused. Therefore, interviews can never replace the value of user observation, whether in a Contextual Inquiry or Usability Test.

While extremely valuable, interviews can be time-consuming to conduct and analyze.

USER SURVEY

What Is This Method?

In a User Survey, users are asked a series of questions that are typically aimed at learning more about a user group or about users' views of a system. Surveys enable design teams to gather a lot of information very quickly which can be statistically analyzed.

When Should It Be Used?

Surveys can be conducted throughout the product lifecycle and can be targeted to the issues that the team is dealing with at any given moment.

How Do You Conduct a User Survey?

In today's wired world, User Surveys tend to be conducted online which is less costly than mail or phone surveys. The online surveys may try to help a product team learn about its users, including demographic information, past

experience with biometric devices, knowledge level with these types of systems, etc. Or, a survey may be more focused on identifying the top issues users have encountered with a system and soliciting ideas for improvement. Whatever the topic of the survey, it is important to design the survey with best practices in survey design in mind. For instance, it is important to ensure the survey does not ask leading questions and to ensure that the length of the survey isn't too long (which may detract some users from completing it).

When designing a survey, it is also important to balance the number of open-ended questions and close-ended questions. Open-ended questions are a wonderful way to gather deeper insights into users' opinions, however these types of questions are difficult and time- consuming to analyze. Additionally, since open-ended questions require more work on the part of the respondent, it is important to note that a survey with too many open-ended questions may prevent users from completing the survey.

Close-ended questions may not offer the same individual insights that open-ended questions do, but they also provide the ability to statistically analyze the data and to perform cross- tabulations with other close-ended questions.

What Are the Benefits/Limitations?

Surveys provide an easy way to gather a lot of data very quickly, yet they suffer from many of the same issues as interviews. Since surveys are asking users to provide opinions and recall experiences, they cannot replace the value of user observation. Additionally, poorly- written surveys can bias design decisions. The data gathered from a survey is only as good as the questions asked. Therefore, it is critical to pilot the survey instrument prior to launching a full-blown survey.

Another issue that can negatively impact the quality of a survey is the sampling methodology. It is important to note, that a survey may not include a representative sample of the user population. Since users have the ability to opt-in or to quit at any time, it is important to review the data to identify segments of the population who are underrepresented. The self-selection nature of surveys makes it extremely difficult to find a truly random sample.

While this technique is certainly more complex than some of the others, the insights that can be learned and the amount of data that can be gathered in a short period of time make this technique a very important part of any design process.

9. CONCLUSION

In today's global society, the use of biometrics to confirm personal identity is a key component to our nation's security. And, as such, there is an escalating need to design *usable and intuitive* biometric systems which accurately identify individuals.

To date, the design of the biometric systems has focused primarily on the effectiveness of a device, including system performance, functionality, reliability and precision. As technology evolves and the performance of these devices improves, it is critical to turn our attention to designing truly usable, user-friendly biometric devices.

Ensuring Successful Biometric Systems

In order to ensure the continued success of biometric systems and devices, it is critical the traditional product development process evolve into a user-centric model that takes into consideration the essential role users play in the biometric process. By understanding the partnership between biometric systems and users, we can begin to have a substantial impact on the design of these systems, including:

- Improved ease-of-use
- Reduced product complexity
- Enhanced system performance
- Increased user satisfaction

By focusing on these attributes, biometric designers can improve the usability of their devices, and as a result, may also improve system performance and throughput, resulting in a significant return on investment, including:

- Increased accuracy and reduced errors
- Decreased time to capture an acceptable sample
- Improved productivity and fewer attempts required
- Reduced need for assistance from system operators
- Decreased support and training costs

Thus, usability improvements not only lead to better, easier-to-use products, they can also lead to substantial cost savings as a result of improved system performance.

Usability and Biometric Systems

In order to improve the usability of biometric systems and reap the benefits of improved system performance, it is critical to take a holistic approach in which users are a key component in the design of a biometric system. By adopting a user-centered design process, wherein users become our design partners and have an integral role in the development of a biometric system, we can begin to have a measurable impact on a system's ease of use.

In this handbook, we've introduced some of the key concepts of this user-centered design lifecycle, including:

- Defining the **Context of Use**
  Including operational environment, user characteristics, tasks, and social environment

- Determining the **User & Organizational Requirements**
  Including business requirements, user requirements, and technical requirements

- Developing the **Design Solution**
  Including the system design, user interface, and training materials

- Conducting the **Evaluation**
  Including usability, accessibility, and conformance testing

While this handbook introduced some of the key user-centered design and usability concepts, it is only meant to be an introduction to a topic that has the potential to significantly improve the future of biometric systems. We've provided a basic outline and some key methods which will help biometric system designers begin to incorporate usability throughout their product lifecycles. But, this is only a start: additional research in the field of usability and biometrics is greatly needed.

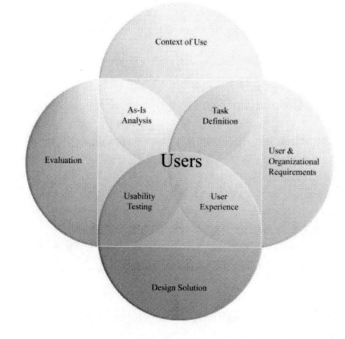

Figure 13. Biometric User-Centered Design Process

At the National Institute of Standards and Technology, we've created the Usability and Biometrics effort which is dedicated to providing resources, such as this handbook, in order to advance biometrics and usability research. In addition to promoting the benefits of usability, we are working to conduct research on how users' interactions and characteristics affect the success of biometric devices, so that we may better understand these issues and their implications for the design of a system.

In an effort to improve the design of biometric technologies, we encourage others to conduct and share their research in this emerging area so that we can continue to improve the usability and ease-of-use of these systems and advance the future of biometric technologies.

WORKS CITED

Biometrics and Usability. (2007). Retrieved from Biometrics and Usability: http://zing.ncsl.nist.gov/biousa/

ISO 13401:1999. *Human-centered design process for interactive systems.*

ISO/IEC 25062:2006. Retrieved from International Organization of Standardization's Software engineering -- Software product Quality Requirements and Evaluation (SQuaRE) -- Common Industry Format (CIF) for usability test reports: http://www.iso.org/iso/ iso_catalogue/ catalogue_tc/ catalogue_detail.htm?csnumber=43046

National Science and Technology Council, (2006). *The National Biometrics Challenge.*

Nielsen, J. *Ten Usability Heuristics.* Retrieved from Useit.com: http://www.useit.com/papers/heuristic

Norman, D. (1988). *The Design of Everyday Things.* New York, New York: Doubleday.

Theofanos, M., Micheals, R., Scholtz, J., Morse, E., & May, P. (2006). Does Habituation Affect Fingerprint Quality? . *Proceedings of ACM SIGCHI Annual Conference.* Montreal, Quebec, Canada.

Theofanos, M., Stanton, B., Michaels, R., & Orandi, S. Biometric Systematic Uncertainity and the User.

End Notes

[1] These tests were supported by the Department of Homeland Security . Specific hardware and software products identified in this report were used in order to perform the evaluations described. In no case does such identification imply recommendation or endorsement by the National Institute of Standards and Technology, nor does it imply that the products and equipment identified are necessarily the best available for the purpose

[2] Please see the section on Usability Research Methods for more detail on each of the methods listed above.

[3] Please see the section on Usability Research Methods for more detail on each of the methods listed above.

CHAPTER SOURCES

The following chapters have been previously published:

Chapter 1 – This is an edited, reformatted and augmented version of a United States Department of Commerce, Technology Administration, National Institute of Standards and Technology publication, NISTIR 7540, dated September 2008.

Chapter 2 – This is an edited, reformatted and augmented version of a United States Department of Commerce, Technology Administration, National Institute of Standards and Technology publication, dated June 11, 2008.

INDEX